The Ubuntu God

Princeton Theological Monograph Series

K. C. Hanson, Charles M. Collier, and D. Christopher Spinks,
Series Editors

Recent volumes in the series:

Mary Clark Moschella
*Living Devotions: Reflections on Immigration, Identity,
and Religious Imagination*

Linden J. DeBie
*Speculative Theology and Common-Sense Religion:
Mercersburg and the Conservative Roots of American Religion*

Michael S. Hogue
*The Tangled Bank: Toward an Ecotheological Ethics
of Responsible Participation*

Charles Bellinger
The Trinitarian Self: The Key to the Puzzle of Violence

Philip Ruge-Jones
*Cross in Tensions: Luther's Theology of the Cross
as Theolgico-social Critique*

Gabriel Andrew Msoka
*Basic Human Rights and the Humanitarian Crises
in Sub-Saharan Africa: Ethical Reflections*

Paul S. Chung et al., editors
*Asian Contextual Theology for the Third Millennium:
Theology of Minjung in Fourth-Eye Formation*

The Ubuntu God
Deconstructing a South African Narrative of Oppression

SAMUEL A. PAUL

☙PICKWICK *Publications* • Eugene, Oregon

THE UBUNTU GOD
Deconstructing a South African Narrative of Oppression

Princeton Theological Monograph Series 101

Copyright © 2009 Samuel A. Paul. All rights reserved. Except for brief quotations in critical articles or reviews, no part of this book may be reproduced in any manner without prior written permission from the publisher. Write: Permissions, Wipf and Stock Publishers, 199 W. 8th Ave., Suite 3, Eugene, OR 97401.

Pickwick Publications
A Division of Wipf and Stock Publishers
199 West 8th Avenue, Suite 3
Eugene, Oregon 97401

www.wipfandstock.com

ISBN 13: 978-1-55635-510-3

Cataloging-in-Publication data:

Paul, Samuel A.

The Ubuntu God : deconstructing a South African narrative of oppression / Samuel A. Paul.

Princeton Theological Monograph Series 101

viii + 186 p. ; 23 cm. Includes bibliographical references

Eugene, Ore.: Pickwick Publications

ISBN 13: 978-1-55635-510-3

1. South Africa. Truth and Reconciliation Commission. 2. Reconciliation—Religious aspects—Christianity—History of doctrines—20th century. 3. Apartheid—South Africa. 4. Apartheid—Religious aspects—Christianity. 5. Liberation theology. 6. South Africa—Church history—20th century. 7. South Africa—Politics and government—1948–1994. 8. South Africa—Politics and government—1994–. I. Title. II. Series.

DT1757 .P38 2009

Manufactured in the U.S.A.

Contents

Acknowledgments / vii

Abbreviations / viii

Introduction / 1

1. The Biblical Basis of Apartheid: A Narrative Analysis of a Community of Believers; Struggling to Make Sense of Faith / 13

2. Deconstructing Oppressive Narratives: The Case of Co-opting Paul / 58

3. Discovering an African Meta-Narrative: Ubuntu Liberation / 84

4. Impact of a New Narrative: A Negotiated Settlement; Truth for Reconciliation / 113

5. From Apartheid's Christian Hegemony to Religious Pluralism / 140

6. Conclusion: A Narrative Analysis of a Faith Journey / 172

Afterword / 176

Bibliography / 179

Acknowledgments

FIRST, I ACKNOWLEDGE THE POLITICAL ACTIVISTS AND FAMILIES WHO underwent imprisonment, interrogations, house arrests, beatings, exile, and the ultimate sacrifice of death, to pursue democracy in South Africa. Their perseverance and conviction led to the fulfillment of their goal on April 4, 1994 when South Africans all over the world cast their votes to elect Nelson Mandela president.

I am grateful for R. D. Naidoo, an uncle of mine. Known as "RD" to all his comrades, he spent most of his life banned as a political activist and under house arrest for his clandestine work with trade unions and the South African Communist Party. As a child, I remember visiting his home and wondering why only my parents were allowed to visit with him for a few minutes in his room with the door slightly cracked open so we could get a brief glimpse of him while my siblings and I waited in the lounge. After finishing high school, I could not afford to go to college, my father negotiated a job for me with RD. Working as a bookkeeper, I soon learned that I was keeping the books for banned underground trade unions in Durban, South Africa, and my politicization and recognition of the evils of apartheid began. Thank you, RD, for opening my eyes; I wish you were alive to know what an impact you made on my life and how you influenced this research project.

To my colleagues at the University of Southern California's Center for Religion and Civic Culture, thank you for all your support in affording me the time and funds toward this project. To Alison Lowell, graduate student and research assistant at USC, who spent weeks formatting and preparing the manuscript to meet publisher deadlines, your assistance was invaluable, thank you so much.

Finally, Eva Peters and Malathi Benjamin, without your help, support, and encouragement throughout the journey, this book would not have been possible. Thank You!

Abbreviations

AFM	Apostolic Faith Mission
ANC	African National Congress
BYULR	*Brigham Young University Law Review*
DRC	Dutch Reformed Church
JChSt	*Journal of Church and State*
JRBS	*Journal of Religion and Behavioral Sciences*
JSNTSup	Journal for the Study of the New Testament: Supplement Series
JTSA	*Journal of Theology for Southern Africa*
NGK	Nederduitse Gereformeerde Kerk
NovT	*Novum Testamentum*
NTS	*New Testament Studies*
NP	Afrikaner National Party
PRSt	*Perspectives in Religious Studies*
SEAJT	*South East Asia Journal of Theology*
ThTo	*Theology Today*
TRC	Truth and Reconciliation Commission
WBC	Word Biblical Commentary

Introduction

I awoke early on the morning of April 4, 1994, a day that I had waited with great expectation for more than three decades. Dressing in a hurry I left the house with a sense of urgency in order to beat the Los Angeles rush hour traffic and position myself in front of a very long line of people at the South African consulate. On this special day I, a Colored South African of Indian descent, would cast my vote for the first time and participate in the electoral process of a free and democratic South Africa.

In the early hours of that momentous morning South Africans living in California gathered at the South African consulate in Beverly Hills, not to voice any protest but to add a new chapter to the books of history. Words could not express the emotions that overcame us as we realized that we, the Colored and Black citizens of South Africa, would finally belong to a place, a people group, a culture and gain or regain our sense of identity. Despite the fact that we were casting our vote in California we finally belonged to the country of our birth, as full citizens of South Africa. Thank you Nelson Mandela, Walter Sisuli, Ahmed Katrada, Govan Mbeki and all those who fought, struggled, faced imprisonment and died for that day. Out of this struggle came liberation for all, for me and my fellow Black and Colored South African brothers and sisters. I got to vote that day. I was now recognized and acknowledged as a democratic free citizen of South Africa. Later that evening I was overwhelmed with tears of unutterable joy as I watched news coverage of the day. I watched myself on television sharing thoughts of my identity with a reporter. It was an unfolding of my African Indian Christian narrative which had always been rather confusing to say the least. I was no longer "just" an Indian who was born in South Africa because the British shipped my great-grandparents there in the early 1860s to toil as slave laborers on sugarcane plantations. Because I was not a citizen of India I was not Indian, and yet, because I was not White I wasn't South African. Just as the Afrikaner was a Christian, I was a Christian, too. Yet in the South Africa of old that did not give me any equal or fair standing despite the New Testament assurance that we are all equal in Christ. So, who am I really? Why is my narrative so different to that of my fellow Afrikaner citizens? How could the Afrikaner find support for apartheid in the Biblical text? These questions and many more have plagued me for most of my life like a demon possessing my thoughts. I embarked on this project in an attempt to fully understand this Afrikaner narrative and to make sense of my very own meta-narrative. Through this study I intend to expose the Afrikaner's oppressive self-serving religious narrative of apartheid with 1948 as my starting point until the events leading to the formation of the Truth and Reconciliation Commission in 1996.

In 1948, the Afrikaner Nationalist Government became the ruling party in South Africa. Under its rule, the political and legal system was noted for its totalitarian interference in the affairs of people's private lives. A policy of "separate developments" was introduced in which the government restricted the freedom of Blacks.[1] Apartheid, the separation of, and discrimination against people based solely on the color of their skin, was introduced. The state determined where people lived, where they could own property, who they could marry, which schools they could attend, and what jobs could be performed by what races. The state dictated which sport clubs people could join, and against whom they could compete. The state regulated which hospitals people could attend, and dictated that blood transfusions were permitted only within one's own race. The state stipulated which church people could attend, and at death, where they could be buried. Apartheid was in total opposition to basic human rights.[2]

The term apartheid literally means "apart-ness" or "separate-ness." It gave a minority regime, elected by one small section of the population, an explicit mandate to govern in the interests, and for the benefit

---

1. The use of racial and ethnic labels as "Coloreds," for people of mixed historical origins (9%), "Indians" or "Asians," for descendants of indentured laborers and traders from the Indian subcontinent (3%); and "Africans" or "Blacks" for the Bantu-speaking majority (76%), given the history of South Africa is problematic. Therefore, the term "Blacks" will be utilized in this study to refer to members of all three "non-White" groups. However, when reference is specifically made to that particular race group, the indigenous Black will be referred to as "African" even though this does not imply that others have not also become Africans through longtime residence and subjective identification.

2. Van der Vyver, "Constitutional Perspective," 635.

of the White community. Such a policy was hostile to the common good of people as a whole, denied the fact that all human beings were made in the image of the Creator, and failed to acknowledge equal dominion over the earth for all.

Christianity has always been a dominant influence in South Africa. Afrikaners drew heavily on Christian scripture and the Christian tradition to weave a self-justifying religious narrative that supported their oppressive ideologies, prohibiting inclusion and suppressing pluralism. At the same time, the focus of the Black Church during this time was to develop and assert a theology that insisted that equality and democracy were attainable, amidst discrimination, brutality, intimidation, violence, poverty, imprisonment and loss. Indeed, in 1990, Nelson Mandela was released from almost 28 years of imprisonment for his active political resistance against the apartheid government. His release indicated that the totalitarian government could no longer maintain its policy of apartheid. After four years of intense negotiations between the Afrikaner National Party (NP) and the African National Congress (ANC), South Africa became a democracy in 1994 and Nelson Mandela was inaugurated as the country's first Black President.

It is a historical fact that the apartheid government abused its power, and participated in some of the world's most atrocious human rights violations. It did so while maintaining its ideological justification of a Christian narrative. The ANC, on the other hand, a Marxist influenced party, led the country to democracy through the medium of Ubuntu as seen in the processes of the Truth and Reconciliation Commission (TRC), utilizing the fundamental Christian principles of confession, repentance, forgiveness, and reconciliation for the purpose of healing and building the nation.

The struggle for racial freedom and liberation in South Africa took place, in part, on a discursive level. Though liberation struggles throughout the world have been forced to grapple with the self-justifying myths of their oppressive regimes, I believe this was truer in South Africa than elsewhere. This project begins with an interrogation of the Afrikaner-Christian narrative that provided the ideological underpinnings for apartheid. I point to the shaky biblical basis of this narrative, specifically to its untenable over-reliance on Romans 13:1-4. Then, I demonstrate how this self-justifying, exclusivist narrative began to unravel through the struggle for liberation in South Africa, an unraveling that both paralleled and was inspired by a global movement within Christian theology originating in the Third World that challenged all versions of colonialist Christianity. The unraveling of the Afrikaner-Apartheid Christian narrative represented the breaking open of religious discourse in the public arena and allowed for a multiplicity of religious narratives, voices, and stories to emerge. This process of "story telling" culminated in 1996 with the TRC, which sought to bring healing through full and honest disclosure of culpability.

In this project I identify this discursive shift from "singularity" of narrative to "plurality" as Ubuntu, an African word meaning humanity to others, and more fully defined later. Though one might engage the topic of Ubuntu from a cultural, anthropological, or sociological perspective, I employ the term "theological." That is, I point to the spirit of Ubuntu at work in the South African context. I identify Ubuntu as a powerful, autonomous *force* in the dismantling of apartheid, and a *spirit* radically present at the TRC.

As part of the negotiations, in exchange for power, the NP wanted blanket amnesty for the crimes committed during its tragic period of apartheid and asked for a Reconciliation Commission to be established. The ANC, on the other hand, wanted a Truth Commission. One was interested in the perpetrators of the crimes generated by apartheid, and the other was concerned with the victims of the apartheid regime. In 1995, the ANC initiated TRC, which sought truth and offered reconciliation.

Apartheid and the TRC were both rooted in the Biblical story. Apartheid united the concepts of manifest destiny and redemptive violence to support a divisive culture of suppression of the majority by a minority. In contrast the ANC conveyed Ubuntu through the TRC by adopting the Biblical stories of prophetic justice and transformative justice through repentance and forgiveness, to bring about unification and to invite reconciliation. These competing concepts are the reverse sides of the same theological reality, which is that manifest destiny (entitlement) is the reverse of prophetic justice, and redemptive violence is the reverse of transformative justice. The Constantinian commitment to extending the Kingdom of God in the nation, which empowered the Reformed theology of the Afrikaner tradition, created the national seedbed for planting a commission inclusive of all groups. Where the parochial, racial, exclusive, and narrow view of redemptive justice prevailed, the TRC sought transformative justice.

Much scholarly work has been done on apartheid in the past fifty years, and most recently on the TRC. However, I offer a unique emphasis both on narrative during apartheid and on the role of Ubuntu during the liberation process.

The methodology utilized in this study is African Narrative Theology. I have chosen this theological methodology because it offers an inclusive and integrative way of addressing issues of culture, class, racial exploitation, oppression, and poverty. African Narrative Theology is deeply rooted in African culture, and more specifically, in the extensive resources of the oral tradition communicated through stories within the South African culture.

Stories provide the fertile soil of South African religions because they bud, grow and flower with deep spiritual, theological, and philosophical insights and visions of humanness. Historically, storytelling has formed the bridge between traditional African religiosity, the African worldview and the Hebrew and Christian Scriptures. Narrative theology, as it brings together the wisdom of oral tradition, transmitted history, and lived experience of morality, community and humanity, provides a broader and more inclusive socio-political account of the South African story and its theological meaning and is, therefore, the most appropriate and useful method for this study. This project is also grounded in several key premises.

First, the South African historical, political, social, economic, cultural, and theological context is best understood and interpreted through the vision of Ubuntu philosophy, theology, and thought. Ubuntu is an African philosophy and way of life. Ubuntu, a word deriving from the Nguni languages, expresses the very high value of human worth which is found within African societies, and conveys a concept of humanism rooted not in western individualism but in a communal context. It is a concept expressive of a culture that places emphasis on communality and on the interdependence of the members of a community; a concept which conveys the belief that each individual's humanity is truly expressed through his or her relationship with others and theirs in turn through a recognition of his or her humanity.[3] Sociolinguist Buntu Mfenyana argues that to understand fully the word Ubuntu one must separate the prefix *ubu* from the root *ntu*:

---

3. Horwitz, "Truth Commissions," 5.

> Ntu is an ancestor who got human society going. He gave us our way of life as human beings. It is a communal way of life which says that society must be run for the sake of all. This requires cooperation, sharing, and charity. There should be no widows or orphans left alone—they all belong to someone. If a man does not have a cow, then give him a cow to milk. There should be no deprived person.[4]

Ubu refers to the abstract. So Ubuntu is the quality of being human. It is the quality, or the behavior, of ntu society that is, sharing, charitableness, and cooperation. It is this quality which distinguishes a human creature from an animal or spirit. When you do something that is not humane then you are being like an animal.[5]

Ubuntu, which means "humanity" in Xhosa and "human nature" in Zulu offers the conceptual paradigm of "solidarity as humans with fellow humans," which serves as a spiritual foundation for all South African indigenous cultures. A key phrase that expresses this solidarity is, "a person is a person through other persons."[6] Ubuntu is a corporate and communal way of life that stands in direct opposition to the hierarchical, discriminatory, separatist and systemic class warfare of apartheid. This individualistic either-or reasoning of the apartheid state ignored the communitarian lifestyle of the African ethic. Thus, heinous crimes are the antithesis of Ubuntu. The peaceful transition from hegemony to negotiations for democracy corresponds to the neither-nor ideology, which is deeply rooted in Ubuntu philosophy. It neither left the status quo intact as the reformers had hoped for, nor did it reverse power relations as the revolutionaries had expected. The philosophy of Ubuntu lends to and is consistent with narrative, which is storytelling in a community context.

Second, that apartheid's dominating hegemony forced upon the South African society homogeneity of norms and enforced absolutism in values which denied the full human dignity, the moral integrity, the historical actuality and the essential spirituality of the other. Treatment that is cruel, inhuman or degrading is bereft of Ubuntu. Ubuntu thought demands that one apprehends and appreciates the faith of the religious other; it transcends absolutism and brings to bear the distinct

---

4. As quoted in Sparks, *The Mind*, 14.
5. Sparks, *The Mind*, 14.
6. Horwitz, "Truth Commissions," 5.

South African sensibility of respect for and treatment of human beings as "being-with-others" and it offers a new definition of what "being-with-others" shall henceforth be about. Ubuntu operates as an ethic of responsibility and reciprocity. It captures how the relation to the other is prior to the self. In other words, one becomes who one is in responding to, and for, the other.[7]

Third, and most important for this project, that the dismantling of apartheid led to recognition of the religious other, the recovery of the alternate narratives of the South African pluralistic and diverse context, that is to the reappearance of Ubuntu perspective and practice in the political and public sphere.

The central theological and moral spine running through the experience of what the Christian Church offered in South Africa can best be described with a string of words linked, like vertebrae, as a social-political-legal-economic-moral-and-theological narrative of the South African experience deconstructed to reveal a movement toward liberation manifest in the following impulses:

- Believers, struggling to make sense of Christian faith in the midst of the old narrative of oppression and separation, finding a transforming principle through a reconciling narrative that reflects elements of Ubuntu thought;
- Interpreters, struggling to make sense of Biblical texts addressing political roles and their ethical realities, finding an alternative African perspective on Romans 13 as a case study;
- Thinkers, struggling to bring together the warring opposites of the past, finding a meta-narrative for South African peoples in the Ubuntu vision which offers a hermeneutics of liberation and a social process for actualizing it in the healing of the sub-nations within a nation;
- Leaders, applying pathways and patterns of healing in Ubuntu thought, creating a new narrative of truth telling and reconciling the oppressor and oppressed;
- Religious leaders, finding that the ultimate work of Ubuntu is the creation of a solidarity that reaches beyond a pluralism of coexistence and lays hold of a new narrative of solidarity that

7. Sanders, "Loss of Ubuntu," 5.

embraces diversity, community and inclusivity in the search for a reconciled future.

Elements of Ubuntu principles can be seen as intrinsically present in the South African journey from 1948 through 1994. South Africa is historically unique, theologically instructive and stands as a light to the nations. It is Ubuntu that gave the South African people courage which culminated, not in denial of the horrors of the past, but in amnesty, truthfulness, integrity and a communal collective solidarity in African society that did not allow for the sacrifice of truth or reconciliation. It was Ubuntu that led them from a hopeless situation of exploitation and abuse to communal solidarity. This powerful thread and need for tribal connectivity in African culture is a sense of truth that is far more existential and a relational necessity than the Afrikaner's idea of transcendent universal truth and its long history of relational exclusivism. The African hope for relational inclusivism was the only solution that brought this country together. Ubuntu brought out the best of both and forced them to face the worst of both. This is a larger and wider universal justice. It was not an either/or, or a both/and, but a neither/nor as seen in the TRC. Though typically the TRC is interpreted in Christian language and motifs, I explore here the ways in which the TRC was, in fact, Ubuntu at work in its true African way.

This project will also touch on how opposing sides used the same Reformed Christian theology. One side used this theology to oppress, while the other used it to liberate, heal, and build a broken nation. South Africa dominated world news for five decades. It has intrigued researchers because it provides a good model to political governments facing the difficult transition to peaceful and amicable change. Certainly, it provides a fascinating example for countries that face difficult change through peaceful negotiations.

I believe this project is important to Christianity in South Africa and elsewhere in its encouragement to fight injustice, be true to the interpretation of scripture, and work faithfully toward healing and reconciliation. This work hopes to contribute to the discipline of Practical Theology and the ongoing dialogue between Christians, religious pluralists, and public policy makers. It also aims to be political and could be described as a study in political theology.

Chapter one presents an examination of the historical context from which the Afrikaner-Christian Apartheid narrative emerged and found its origins. In particular this context was one in which different races had been in conflict for nearly three-and-a-half centuries culminating in first the rise and then the crisis of apartheid.

The first chapter also addresses the arrival of the Dutch in the mid-1650s and of the British in the 1820s who in turn brought in Indians as migrant workers for cheap labor. It focuses on the struggle for power, dominance, and land first between the indigenous peoples of South Africa and the Afrikaners, and thereafter between the Afrikaners and the British, with the Indians and so-called Coloreds sandwiched between the Afrikaners and British, with absolutely no power at all. The first Anglo-Boer War (1877-1881) brought into power the British who had already set the foundations for racial discrimination, which the Afrikaner brilliantly shaped and orchestrated after the victory over the British in the second Anglo-Boer War (1899-1902), a victory that eventually led to the creation of the National Party in 1914. When the National Party came into power in 1948, apartheid, which had already existed in various forms for several hundred years, became the platform on which the Afrikaners initially campaigned and subsequently instituted as law to solidify their victory.

The Afrikaners justified a policy of apartheid both before and after 1948 by drawing upon a religious narrative, which declared they were the chosen people of God, the *volk*. They proceeded along a path of maintaining this *volk* and choseness through the implementation of various laws racially segregating Black South Africans. Thus, Chapter one explores some of the laws of apartheid and the ideological and narrative backing of these laws through scripture and the Dutch Reformed Church. At the same time, in this first chapter, I introduce other Christian voices which were opposed to apartheid and the National Party.

The chapter concludes with a description of one of the fundamentalist churches of South Africa, namely the Apostolic Faith Mission (AFM), which was divided into the four race groupings: White, Black, Indian, and Colored. After decades of attempts by the Black section of this church to unite and operate as one body, in 1990 the AFM accomplished that milestone. This is a remarkable event in that one of the most theologically conservative Pentecostal churches became the first denomination to reach a decision to unite and work as one multiracial entity. In keeping with the sentiment of racial healing and reconciliation, this was an indication that the church in South Africa once again set the momentum for the country and was prophetic as to what was to be experienced by all South Africans four years later; Ubuntu at work in a new Democracy.

Chapter two interrogates one of the central biblical underpinnings for the Afrikaners' origin myth/narrative that they had a covenantal destiny as the chosen race to carry out God's plans and purposes for the future of South Africa. I have already suggested that they leaned on the Bible for guidance and direction. However, Romans 13:1–4 became the most essential text to support the Afrikaners' view of covenantal destiny as a mandate to rule South Africa unswervingly and faithfully. In chapter two I propose alternate contexts in which Paul may have written this letter in order to challenge the Afrikaner-Christian narrative. Mine is not the traditional reading of Romans 13 but rather an alternative reading intended to re-appropriate Paul so as to deconstruct South Africa's oppressive narrative by challenging the Afrikaner interpretation and misappropriation of Romans 13 to support its oppressive rule on another group, Blacks, within the same community of belief.

In chapter three, I explore how, in the fight for liberation, a Black South African community of believers struggled to make sense of the Christian faith, and discovered a new African meta-narrative of liberation by drawing from other oppressive contexts globally. What is explored in this chapter is not a top-down model, nor a representation of scripture that supports an oppressive model, but rather a model that liberates and supports equality, humanity, dignity, and integrity the Ubuntu way. Chapter three surveys some dominant liberation hermeneutical trajectories in the, so-called, two-thirds world contexts of Latin America, Asia, and Africa. These counter-narratives within the Christian tradition represented an opening up of the Christian discourse to multiple voices, creating new narrative possibilities for the South African struggle. Chapter three looks at liberation theology from the Latin American perspective, minjung theology from the Asian perspective, and African theologies. First, it provides a critique of hermeneutics that leads to a section on why context is necessary for interpretation. The model presented in this chapter is that of a multiple conversation, recognizing that interpreters are drawn to texts that address issues specific to their contexts. One of the essential elements in exegesis is that the interpreter must always approach and analyze a text within its context: historical, cultural, geographical, ecclesiastical, ideological, or literary. There is a definite context to every text.

Chapter four deals with how South Africa accomplished national healing through the TRC. I argue that the TRC drew on the narrative openings created by the struggle against apartheid, and by global anti-colonial theological movement, and created a platform for multiple voices, stories, and religious narratives to be shared in a public political context. After Nelson Mandela took office as President in 1994, the question that dominated South African politics was how the new government would deal with the human rights violations of the previous regime. As part of the negotiation process for democracy, the outgoing National Party wanted a blanket amnesty for the perpetrators of apartheid crimes. The African National Congress however, wanted a Truth Commission. The ANC's goal was for a peaceful transition to democracy, with the desire to reconcile with its former enemies and bring healing to a scarred and fragile nation.

Ubuntu, the liberating African theology which sustained the hope of the Black community throughout decades of oppression by White rule, is put into action within the process of the TRC where individual and retributive justice is bargained and negotiated for restorative and communal justice in the interests of reconciliation, national healing and nation building. The impact of Ubuntu was that it provided an opportunity, a forum, and a place for people to come and tell their narratives. Stories of hate, love, murder, obedience, resistance, kidnapping, detention, corruption, deceit, confession, repentance, forgiveness, and reconciliation were all told for South Africa to hear, for the world to listen to, for a remembering back into one society, a community struggling to make sense of faith. Chapter four reviews how the TRC brought about reconciliation and healing in its attempt to provide a safe place for people to tell their stories so that the nation as a whole, and the entire world, could listen.

Where formerly elitist and exclusivist narratives appropriated from Christianity were used to support apartheid, chapter five reviews the principles that now govern church-state relationships and shows that there is no separation of church and state. The state confidently seeks to uphold neutral religious practices in conformity with the egalitarian foundations of its new constitution. It is not a secular state either because religion is not perceived as taboo. In this chapter I will examine, evaluate, and compare the American establishment and free exercise clauses over against the 1996 South African Constitution and other African countries' constitutional provisions relating to religious freedom.

Chapter five will show how the new South Africa attempts to Africanize the country, moving away from the Western and European narratives of elitism and exclusion which only benefited the White elite minority. It will show how the new South Africa seeks to uphold African values of community and inclusion in its institutions, particularly in its new Constitution of April 1996. This document, which itself can be read as one of these new narratives, was constructed to eliminate hegemony and provide social, political, and legal structures that are open to a multiplicity of religious narratives and stories. This new Constitution set the foundation for a peaceful transition from oligarchy to democracy. A transitional Constitution enforced in April 27, 1994, served as a bridge between the repressive, unjust, and painful past, and a peaceful, democratic, multi-narrative future. The 1996 Constitution was enacted in February 1997. It sought to foster affirmative tolerance, by which people make an effort to understand, accept, and appreciate one another, rather than a passive tolerance, which promotes the apathetic attitude of people just putting up with one another. Further, Chapter five will show how the new Constitution aims at a high level of affirmative tolerance, because it foresees an embracing of otherness.

Provisions are made for particularities that arise out of a diversity of religious individuals and communities. Reconciliation is a high priority for South Africa as it engages in nation building, and therefore the preamble of the final Constitution addresses the importance of, and promotes positive or affirmative, tolerance. The era of the domination of Christian narratives has ended and, as a result, South Africa may well be the strongest democracy in the region. While other African countries' transitions to full democracy have stagnated, South Africa has been able to maintain its progression toward democracy with its changes in religious freedom, its openness to multiple religious narratives, and other guarantees of fundamental human rights.[8]

---

8. du Plessis, "Freedom," 3-4.

1

The Biblical Basis of Apartheid

A Narrative Analysis of a Community of Believers Struggling to Make Sense of Faith

> Change does not roll in on the wheels of inevitability. It comes through the tireless efforts and hard work of those who are willing to take the risk of fighting for freedom, democracy, and human dignity.
>
> —Allan Boesak[1]

Historical Background

THE AFRIKANERS' NARRATIVE WAS SHAPED AROUND A STRONG CONVICTION that they were the chosen people of God, or *volk*. With roots deep in the colonial period, their self-justifying mythology entered the twentieth century aimed at preserving this *volk* and choseness with meta-narratives of racial segregation of the Black South African. This chapter explores the origins of this self-justifying mythology, in particular the Dutch Reformed Church's appeal to scripture and its eventual support of the laws of apartheid. But here I also treat counter-narratives to this mythology, addressing Christian voices that were opposed to apartheid and the National Party in the twentieth century. The chapter concludes with an analysis of one of the fundamentalist Pentecostal churches of South Africa namely the Apostolic Faith Mission (AFM) which was divided into the four race groupings, the White, Black, Indian, and the Colored group.

After decades of attempts by the Black section of the church, the AFM finally decided to unite and operate as one body in 1990. This was

---

1. As quoted in Kendall and Louw, *After Apartheid*, 187.

a demonstration of Ubuntu at work in that one of the most theologically conservative churches became the first denomination to decide to unite and work as one multiracial entity. This was symbolic of the fact that the church in South Africa was responsible for setting the momentum of the country as a whole and was prophetic of what was to be experienced by all South Africans four years later, Ubuntu working together in a new Democracy.

In the spirit of the theme of narrative that anchors this project both theoretically and methodologically, I offer a fable from Joseph Barndt's *Dismantling Racism* that illuminates the South African struggle with a powerful light:

> Once upon a time there was a kingdom of people who pursued happiness. Nothing was more important to them than being happy. The happier they became, the happier they wanted to be. The source of the people's happiness was a magic Happiness Machine. Whenever the people felt unhappy they would pour their troubled feelings into the Happiness Machine. The magic machine would melt their feelings down and purify them. The residue of their troubles became dross, and the dross was drained away and dumped into a distant part of the Kingdom. The people would take their purified feelings and go away singing and feeling happy again. The years and centuries went by, and the happy people became happier and happier because of the wonderful effects of the Happiness Machine.
>
> There was only one problem. Another group of people lived in a distant part of the kingdom where all the dross was dumped. The dross made them very unhappy. And the more dross that was dumped, the unhappier they became. Unfortunately, these poor, unhappy people were not permitted to use the Happiness Machine, because the one thing the magic machine could not do was purify its own dross.
>
> The unhappy people complained to the happy people about the problems they had with the dross. But the happy people ignored their complaints. When they were confronted with the terrible results of their happiness, these happy people simply took their troubled feelings to their Happiness Machine and it made them happy again. It was easy to believe that it was not the dross of their own troubles that made other people unhappy. Rather, they convinced themselves that the unhappy people were just incurably unhappy and they had nobody but themselves to blame for their unhappiness.

It was not long before the unhappy people began to protest more insistently about their situation. They organized marches and demonstrations. They demanded that the dross be removed from their part of the kingdom. And they demanded a fair share of happiness for their people. But the happy people turned a deaf ear to their protests, which only served to make the unhappy people angrier, and they protested all the more.

Finally, the happy people could no longer ignore the protests. They used force to put down the protesters, and arrested and jailed the leaders. They passed laws and organized military force to control the unhappy people. Many of the unhappy people were killed. This only made the others angrier and unhappy. They began to plot and plan how they could destroy the Happiness Machine.

The conflict and tension caused a severe drain on the happy people's happiness. In addition to everything else, many of them were becoming uneasy about the way the unhappy people were being treated. All these new troubles made the Happiness Machine work even harder, and consequently, even more dross was produced. They had to build an even bigger and better Happiness Machine to take care of the happiness needs of the people; consequently, the dross was piled higher and higher and spread farther and farther into other parts of the kingdom, which made more and more people unhappy and angry. It was not long before the unhappy people were in a constant state of rebellion.

Then a new and even greater danger arose. The Happiness Machine became so large and productive that there was no place on earth left to put the dross. The piles of dross crept closer and closer to the homes of the happy people and to the place where the Happiness Machine was operating. Now the happy people were threatened not only by the rebellion of the unhappy people, but also by their own Happiness Machine.

The new danger caused even greater internal conflict and tension among the happy people. Some wanted to build an even bigger Happiness Machine in order to deal with the crisis they were facing. Others began to see that the Happiness Machine was not the solution to their problems, but the cause. They wanted to reduce the size of the machine, or even dismantle it altogether. Some even began to wish that they could join together with the unhappy people to find solutions to the problem and build a new society together.[2]

---

2. Barndt, *Dismantling*, 1–3.

This is the story of South Africa until 1994, when for the first time in its history both the happy people, (White people), and the unhappy people, (Black people), joined together to find solutions to their fractured community. Together they combined to build a new society, working toward a unified community that would live together harmoniously.

The chapter begins by offering a historical background of Dutch origins in the Cape. Next, it discusses the church's role and involvement in the struggle for human rights, with reference to, and in light of, the historical foundation previously lain. It specifically deals with the struggle against the policy of Apartheid and the Afrikaners' justification for it biblically. Finally, through an examination of the National Conference of churches in South Africa in 1990, and the subsequent changes implemented by the Apostolic Faith Mission Church of S.A., the current move toward a harmonious community is explored.

The Khoisan Presence and the Dutch Invasion of the Cape

The Afrikaners directly narrated their historical experience in light of Biblical texts and stories in which they understood themselves as God's chosen people. This engagement with biblical texts lent them a framework from which they interpreted both their experience as *voortrekkers* and the battle at Blood River. To begin with, there is a long-standing narrative among White South Africans that the iron-working Bantu crossed the Limpopo River into southern Africa sometime during the 17th century. This belief supports the idea that Whites were the first to settle South Africa. This is the foundation of the belief that White settlers entered an "empty land" in the 17th and 18th centuries, scattered with just a few Khoikhoi pastoralists.[3] The settlers commonly referred to the Khoisan as "Hottentots" or "Bushmen." "Hottentot" is defined in the Oxford Dictionary as, "a person of inferior intellect or culture," and in the Dutch dictionary as, "a rough, unmannerly person."[4] This

---

3. The indigenous African will be referred to as Khoisan in this chapter. Khoisan is defined by Webster's Dictionary as "a group of African peoples speaking Khoisan languages, a subfamily of African languages of Hottentot and the several languages known as Bushman and related to Sandawe and Hasta with which it forms the Macro-Khoisan family." See *Merriam-Webster's Collegiate Dictionary*, 11th ed., s. v. "Khoisan."

4. See reference to dictionaries in Elphick, *Kraal and Castle*, xv. See also *Oxford English Dictionary*, 2nd ed., s. v. "Hottentot."

derogatory labeling helps define the intellectual climate of Europe during that era, an era in which a "Hottentot" was a widely accepted symbol for "irredeemable savagery and the very depths of human degradation."[5] This perspective suited the ruling White minority, and helped justify the unequal ownership of the majority of South African lands. However, this White version of history is more myth than fact. Archaeological and historical research has evidenced an ancient history of Black civilzation in southern Africa.[6]

During the 16th century, European sailing-ships, comprised mainly of Dutch and English traders, made regular voyages around the southern tip of Africa to facilitate trade in India, Southeast Asia, and Indonesia. Europeans commonly knew these lands as the "East Indies." Since the Cape was midway between Europe and Asia, by the 17th century Table Bay had become a regular port for traders. There they paused in their journeys to replenish fresh water and supplies. Meat was bought from the local Khoisan farmers. By the mid-17th century almost 50,000 Khoisan pastoralists were estimated to be living in the region, southwest of the Olifants and Breede rivers. Clans living nearest Table Bay initially welcomed the opportunity to trade their surplus, as well as their sick and old livestock in exchange for copper, iron, beads, and tobacco. Trading goods with the passing ships was easier for the Khoisan than taking part in long distance trading with neighboring clans to the north.[7]

Since the Khoisan were the only suppliers of fresh meat to the Europeans at the Cape, they were able to demand a high price for their livestock. At the same time they were not willing to sell as many livestock as the Europeans wanted. Eventually this led to conflict between the European traders and the Khoisan. European sailors began to attack the Khoisan and seize their animals. They then sailed off with no concern as to how the Khoisan might respond when the next unsuspecting ship stopped to replenish its supplies. In time the Europeans found this arrangement for replenishing supplies in the Cape to be both expensive and unpredictable. Therefore, the Dutch trading monopoly, known as the Dutch East India Company, decided to resolve the problem by

5. Elphick, *Kraal and Castle*, xv.
6. Shillington, *History*, 212.
7. Ibid., 213.

forming a permanent base on the southern shores of the Cape in 1652. The Dutch intended to stabilize the meat trade with the Khoisan, to keep prices down, grow fresh fruit and vegetables, and provide a hospital for sick sailors. In this way, the Dutch monopolized the trade at the Cape, and profited from selling supplies to other ships. They also built a fortress to protect the base from attacks by other European traders. Such was the beginning of the invasion of South African soil by the Dutch, who became known as Afrikaners.[8] The Dutch East India Company obviously had other intentions than just to form a base at Table Bay for meeting the needs of replenishing food supplies for the passing trade ships on their way to do trade in the East. Jan Van Riebeeck, one of the company's commanders and masterminds in the Dutch invasion into the Cape released soldiers from their contracts to set up as independent "Boers," (the Dutch word for farmers). These soldiers were given slave labor brought from West Africa and settled on Khoisan land south of Table Bay which they used to farm and graze their livestock. This marks the first conflict between the Dutch and the Khoisan which led to the first Khoi/Dutch war in 1659. The Khoi, who initially welcomed the opportunity of trade with the Dutch, now regretted the permanent dominant presence of the White settlement. The Dutch became more demanding in their need for cattle from the Khoi with requests for larger numbers than the Khoi were willing to trade. The Dutch, in exchange, were only prepared to offer beads, tobacco, copper, and alcohol. They no longer wanted to trade iron for fear that the Khoisan would use it to make weapons to use against them. Guns were never a part of the trade exchange for the same reason.[9]

8. Ibid., 214–16.

9. The Khoi suffered frequent cattle raids on their farms. If they refused to trade, the Dutch invented excuses such as the theft of tobacco by the Khoi to justify their raids. Van Riebeeck recorded these words in his journal after the war with the Khoi in 1659: "They spoke for a long time about our taking everyday for our own use more of the land which had belonged to them from all ages, and on which they were accustomed to pasture their cattle. They also asked, whether, if they were to come to Holland, they would be permitted to act in a similar manner, saying, 'it would not matter if you stayed at the Fort, but you come into the interior, selecting the best land for yourselves, and never once asking whether we like it, or whether it will put us to any inconvenience.' They therefore insisted very strenuously that they should again be allowed free access to the pasture. They objected that there was not enough grass for both their cattle and ours. 'Are we not right therefore to prevent you from getting more cattle? For, if you get many cattle, you come and occupy our pasture with them, and then say the land is not

The conclusion of the Dutch/Khoisan war left the Dutch undisputed rulers of the Cape Peninsula. The Khoi were allowed to utilize the land for pasture only if it was unoccupied. Jan Van Riebeeck, commander and founder of the first Dutch settlement, (1652–62), found that twenty men on horseback kept the colony borders against Khoisan without fortification. As a further precaution, aimed at keeping the Khoisan from driving out the colonial cattle, he planted hedges of bitter almond and thorn. Thus, Khoisan who wished to come onto the peninsula, were forced to pass through the hedge at certain checkpoints and to use designated routes of pasture. The wild almond has a long blueish leaf and nut encased in a shell which is dry and bitter. Today the trees are the remains of a hedge planted in 1660. It was the first apartheid action in South Africa. By 1662, the Dutch held maximum control over the Khoisan. Van Riebeeck's policies were successful according to Dutch standards. Whether these policies were ever questioned as just, fair, ethical, or right, seems a moot point. Three centuries later, the same methods were used by the Afrikaners to oppress Black South Africans.[10]

What accounting can be given for a social order based on a narrated racism that surfaced in the Cape settlement? According to MacCrone's theory, this social order originated between Christians and non-Christians. MacCrone's view on the conflict maintains that the "frontier" birthed a religious group into a racial group, which then gave rise to a more aggressive color prejudice that filtered down through the entire society.[11]

There is yet another explanation for the belief system of the Afrikaner, rooted in the concept of "primitive Calvinism." In Afrikaner civil religion, God's sovereignty is mustered through the workings of His rule in the affairs of nations. This sentiment is portrayed best in a quote from D. F. Malan, Minister of the Interior from 1924 to 1933:

---

wide enough for us both! Who then, with the greatest degree of justice, should give way, the natural owner, or the foreign invader?' They insisted so much on this point that we told them they had now lost that land in war, and therefore could not expect to get it back. It was our intention to keep it." (Adapted from an extract printed in Moodie, *The Record*, 1:205.)

10. Elphick and Giliomee, *The Shaping*, 115–16.
11. MacCrone, "The Frontier," 19–30.

> Our history is the greatest masterpiece of the centuries. We hold this nationhood as our due for it was given us by the Architect of the universe. His aim was the formation of a new nation among the nations of the world ... The last hundred years have witnessed a miracle behind which must lie a divine plan. Indeed, the history of the Afrikaner reveals a will and a determination which makes one feel that Afrikanerdom is not the work of men but the creation of God.[12]

According to Van Jaarsveld, divine calling is not peculiar but seems to be intrinsic to Afrikaner nationalism. It is perceived that the Christian narrative of mission, election, and calling belongs only to the European nations. Therefore the Voortrekkers' mission was to sow the seeds of Christianity among the barbarians. One concludes that there was a strong desire of Christian responsibility toward the heathen. They saw themselves as instruments of God to civilize the non-White.[13] This elaborate origin myth for Dutch occupation of the Cape shaped their own consciousness and self-understanding, just as it defined and molded the political discourse and public policy of apartheid centuries later.

The Afrikaner saw the British Empire as an incarnation of evil. The Zulu army became God's agents to unite the Afrikaner in a holy covenant with the Creator. God had chosen the Afrikaner for a special destiny. So British oppression and Black threats were an honor to contend with because they were only a seal of God's election to Afrikanerdom as a chosen Volk.[14]

The civil religion that Paul Kruger, president of the South African Republic (1881–1900), formulated in the 1930s was both Calvinist and exclusivist. The way Calvin developed his doctrine of predestination was by embracing the Old Testament idea of an ethnic covenant between God and a chosen people. In this way, one people are peculiarly chosen, while others are rejected. This is clearly articulated in his providential rule that some mothers' breasts will be more liberally full than other mothers' breasts.[15] And Calvin again states on matters of salvation, that

---

12. Moodie, *The Rise*, 1.
13. Van Jaarsveld, "The Afrikaner's Idea," 16–19.
14. Moodie, *The Rise*, 11–12.
15. Calvin, *Institutes* 1.16.3.

those that God passes, he will condemn because he wills to exclude them from the inheritance.[16]

Calvin distinguishes clearly between an individual's "special call" to salvation and the "intermediate election" of an ethnic group who is called to fulfill His purposes. It was with this narrative of "intermediate election" that Kruger applied the doctrine of national covenant to the people of the Republic. For Kruger, the miraculous outcome of the war of 1881 was proof of God's election of the people of the Republic. This became a tenet of Kruger's civil faith that God desired the Afrikaner as a chosen people to remain politically independent.[17] Most Europeans who settled in South Africa in the 17th century were Dutch. As colonialists, they were convinced that they were of a superior culture and religion and, thus, cultural chauvinism was foundational to their movement. They were convinced that a Christian European was superior to a member of any other race and that no Black person, heathen or Christian, could ever be a member of the chosen.[18]

The Great Trek as the Exodus

At the heart of the Afrikaner origin myth is the potent story of their "Great Trek," a historical event that was the consequence of the arrival of British settlers to the Cape. If the Dutch invasion of the Cape seemed unfair, wicked, and intentional, then the British takeover made the Dutch look angelic. At the end of the eighteenth century and at the beginning of the nineteenth, this new usurper arrived to challenge the Dutch monopoly, using advanced experience in the wheeling and dealing game that required deceit, greed, and prejudice.

In 1795, while many European countries had fallen prey to the troops of the French under Napoleon Bonaparte, a host of British warships occupied Simon's Bay on July 9th. On August 7th, British troops supported by gunfire swept along the coast towards Muizenberg. By September 15th, the Dutch garrison was crushed. Almost 150 years of Dutch rule came to a crashing halt. The British, masters at mollifying conquered subjects, won the confidence of their new subjects by including Dutch officials in their new administration. This skillful public

---

16. Ibid., 3.23.1.
17. Moodie, *The Rise*, 22–25.
18. Elphick and Giliomee, *The Shaping*, 362–63.

relations ploy abolished some of the difficult aspects of the trading monopoly enjoyed by the Dutch East India Company.[19]

In an attempt to secure a profitable British colony, the British introduced a number of economic and social changes to the newly claimed territory with the intention that these changes would drive the "Boers" (farmers) northward, out of their settled colony.

At first, the Boers found these changes appealing. Wine farmers enjoyed freer access to the British markets. British ships arrived at the Cape port with increased frequency providing better markets for wheat-farmers and trek-boers of the interior. Trek-Boer hunters benefited both from the expanding British market for African ivory and the Merino sheep grown for wool rather than just for meat.[20]

In 1807, the abolition of the slave trade by the British caused a shortage of labor, a policy that fulfilled the original intent to drive the Boers northward. As the British tightened the control of free labor in the colony, the result was the requirement that all Khoisan and "free-Black" men carry passes showing proof of employment and place of residence. If one was found without a pass, they were contracted to the nearest White colony requiring labor. At this period of time, a number of Christian missionaries arrived from Europe to "Christianize" and "civilize" the so-called "heathen native." Due to their efforts, the Khoisan and "Colored" (a race resulting from interracial sexual activity between the colonialists and the indigenous African) workers were allowed more basic rights and freedom to move and choose their own employer or become independent farmers.[21]

The Khoisan found an important ally in the missionary John Philip. As director of the London Missionary Society, he wielded great influence with British politicians. As a result of his influence the Cape authorities published Ordinance 50 which granted all "Hottentots and other free persons of color," residing in the Cape the same freedoms enjoyed by Whites. This meant that they now could legally own land and were no longer required to carry passes. Much to the dissatisfaction of the Boers, these new laws restricted their use of slave labor and resulted in a strong incentive for the frontier Boers to immigrate into the

---

19. Oakes and Steyn, *Illustrated History*, 94.
20. Shillington, *History*, 266.
21. Ibid., 266–67.

interior beyond the borders of the Cape colony. This was the beginning of what became known in Afrikaner history as the Great Trek inland.[22]

The Great Trek was the Afrikaner exodus from the British Cape Colony frontiers to the interior north and northeast. The Boers would later see the Trek as a repetition of the exodus of the people of Israel and their testing in the wilderness. This was the Afrikaner solution to what they viewed as an intolerable situation in the Cape settlement. The Afrikaner had sustained many severe losses as a result of the wars with the Xhosas, without assistance from the British government. Furthermore, the British government enforced the policy that Blacks deserved equal place in their homes and churches. For the Afrikaner, this was intolerable. An historic document, which became known as Retief's Manifesto, appeared in the *Grahamstown Journal* and is said to explain the main causes of the Great Trek:

> We are resolved, wherever we go, that we will uphold the just principles of liberty ... No-one shall be held in a state of slavery [but we will] preserve proper relations between master and servant ... We will not molest any people, nor deprive them of the smallest property, but if attacked, we shall consider ourselves fully justified in defending our persons and effects ... We make known that when we shall have framed a code of laws for our future guidance, copies shall be forwarded to the colony for general information ... We propose in the course of our journey, and on arriving at the country in which we shall permanently reside, to make known to the native tribes our intentions, and our desire to live in peace and friendly intercourse with them ... We are now quitting the fruitful land of our birth, in which we have suffered enormous losses and continued vexation, and are entering a wild and dangerous territory; but we go with firm reliance on an all-seeing, just, and merciful Being, Whom it will be our endeavors to fear and humbly to obey.[23]

Historically Van Jaarsveld suggests that the Great Trek was the central theme that actually linked the dispersed Afrikaner together as one nation. Even though they were separated in different parts of the country or other corners of the "fatherland" they were still one nation unbroken and this strengthened the national identity. "The Trekkers

---

22. Oakes and Steyn, *Illustrated History*, 97.
23. Kendall and Louw, *After Apartheid*, 28.

had not left an 'English Colony' but their fatherland, and they had not emigrated to 'another land' but to another corner of the fatherland."[24]

The Battle at (Ncome) Blood River

Nowhere is the Afrikaners' narrative of self-justification more pronounced than in their collective recollection of the battle at Blood River. It is here, more than anywhere else, that they have narrated historical events in biblical language and motifs. "This man," declared the widow of slain Voortrekker leader Piet Retief, "has been sent by God. He will help us revenge."[25] This man was Andries Pretorius, a dynamic natural leader who had earned the respect of the Boers. November 1838 was a bleak month for the Voortrekkers' whose goal was to settle in Zululand but who were without a leader. Piet Retief, and his men were murdered by the Zulu chief Dingaan at his kraal (village), during a meeting in which, it was assumed Dingaan would voluntarily cede land to the Voortrekkers. In the wake of Retief's death, Pretorius eventually assumed the role of leader. On December 9th, Pretorius climbed onto a gun carriage and asked his scouts to join him in a vow to God. If God gave them victory over the Zulus he added, "we would note the date of the victory to make it known even to our latest posterity in order that it might be celebrated to the honor of God."[26]

On December 15th, Pretorius' men on guard reported a large Zulu convoy near the Boer holdout. Pretorius commanded the Boers to form a laager camp (a travelers' encampment protected by a circle of wagons, a military encampment or defensive position protected by a ring of armored vehicles), choosing a site between the Ncome River and a deep trench. Wagons were closely tied together with three openings for cannons. Early in the morning of December 16th, the Zulus charged the Boer laager, but their spears were no match for the Boers' muskets and guns. Adopting vocabulary and imagery that is biblical in both scale and scope, one Boer recorded that, "Nothing remains in my memory except shouting and tumult and lamentations."[27] Finally, hundreds of Zulus lay dead, while Pretorius ordered his laager to move out on horseback to

24. Van Jaarsveld, *The Awakening*, 202.
25. Oakes and Steyn, *Illustrated History*, 119.
26. Ibid.
27. Ibid.

finish the destruction of the Zulus. Many Zulus sought refuge in a deep ravine where the Boers shot them. Chaplain Sarel Cilliers recalled later that, "the word of the Lord was fulfilled, by one way shall your enemies come, but by the blessing of the Lord they shall fly before your face." When it was all over, he said, "the Kaffirs lay on the ground like pumpkins on a rich soil that has borne a large crop."[28]

Three thousand Zulus were slain, while only three of the 468 trekkers suffered injury. The Ncome River, flooded with the blood of the Zulus, was thereafter called "Blood River." The Boers perceived this event as God's intervention on their behalf. According to them, God had answered their prayer. Therefore, they vowed that since God granted them the victory, they would honor God and always celebrate that day as the "day of the vow." In 1843, Anna Steenkamp, a Voortrekker living in Natal, wrote a letter to her relatives in the Cape in which she cites the reasons for the Great Trek. She blamed the continued depredations and robberies of the Kaffirs for making life on the eastern frontier unbearable. The emancipation of slaves; "not so much their freedom that drove us to such lengths, but their being placed on an equal footing with Christians, contrary to the laws of God and the natural distinction of race and religion, so that it was intolerable for any decent Christian to bow beneath such a yoke; wherefore we withdrew in order to preserve our doctrines in purity."[29]

The victory at Blood River for the Afrikaner solidified the belief that this exodus was a sign that God had chosen them to rule and lead South Africa, and that they would overcome trials and tribulation such as the Zulus, the British, the Indians, and would soon be the only dominant force freely ruling without opposition.

Arrival of the Indians

When sugar was first produced from cane in Natal in 1851, the colony seemed set for an economic boom. Within seven years the sugar industry was firmly rooted in the colony. However, there was a surfeit of cheap labor. The Zulus were not willing to toil in White-owned fields for any length of time and this prevented a thriving sugar economy. So

---

28. Ibid.
29. de Gruchy, *The Church*, 19.

the farmers search for labor took them throughout the empire, all the way to India.

Natal was not alone in this labor predicament. Since the emancipation of slaves in the British Empire in 1834, other British colonies faced similar labor shortages. The government of India permitted emigration of indentured labor to Mauritius, the West Indies islands, Jamaica, British Guiana, and Trinidad in 1842, to St. Lucia in 1856, and to Granada in 1858. The results of this policy were prosperous sugar economies in these regions. Natal was determined to adopt the same solution. Indian officials under the supervision of a protector of emigrants conducted recruitment. His duties were to supervise emigration, prevent fraudulency, provide pre-embarkation medical inspection, arrange for the safekeeping of the laborers' savings, and prescribe conditions for the return trip of the indentured laborer. Emigration was permitted from only three ports, Madras, Bombay, and Calcutta. A free return passage at the end of a ten-year overseas residence was part of the contract, if the distance from India was further than Mauritius.[30]

Davarum was thirty years old when he put his thumbprint on a document that he could not even read. He had no idea where Natal was, let alone the implications of Act No. 14, but for ten shillings a month, he and hundreds of thousands of his countrymen and women, were prepared to escape the poverty and starvation of India. His thumbprint was consent to a contract that read, "We the adult male emigrants do hereby agree to serve the employer to whom we may respectively be allotted by the Natal Government under the Natal Act No. 14 of 1859 and we all understand the terms under which we are engaged." The contract assigned labor to a particular farmer for an initial period of 3 years which was later amended to five years and then again for another two years. Upon service in Natal for a further five years as a "free" laborer, the immigrants then had the choice of accepting a free return passage to India or remaining in Natal. Between 1860 and 1911, when indentures ceased, 152,000 Indians were estimated to have landed in Natal, with about 52% deciding to remain after serving their contracts.[31]

On October 12, 1860, Davarum, number 1, known as "coolie" ("an unskilled laborer or porter in or from the Far East hired for low or

---

30. Huttenback, *Ghandi*, 2.
31. Oakes and Steyn, *Illustrated History*, 222.

subsistence wages"), his wife, number 2, and their two children, numbers 3 and 4, were among three hundred and thirty eight others at the Madras harbor in India preparing for a long journey to Durban, South Africa. On November 16, 1860, a crowd of White spectators gathered at the Natal Bay to watch the arrival of the "coolies," who were herded by armed police into incomplete barracks without toilets, washing, or cooking facilities. They remained under guard at this place of squalor for eight days while waiting for their prospective employers. Four people died in those wretched conditions.[32]

The farmers were to provide housing for the laborers but upon arrival at the plantations the workers found no accommodations. The workers constructed their own shacks as living quarters and built barracks out of corrugated iron, mud, and stone in which the workers were crammed and uncomfortable, without any form of privacy. Working conditions were appalling. They rose every morning before sunrise to an unappetizing bowl of cold porridge for breakfast, after which they marched to the fields to plant, dig, break new soil, cut, harvest, carry, and build until sunset. Their only break was at midday for another bowl of cold porridge. It was dark by the time they reached their barracks, where they fell into exhausted sleep in preparation to repeat the events of the previous day. Sundays were supposed to be free days but only a few farmers complied. Hospital facilities were inadequate, despite an official requirement that employers with more than twenty laborers had to provide proper facilities to treat the sick. The hospitals crammed men, women, and children together irrespective of the patients' conditions. Latrines consisted of four holes in the ground, without any water basins or baths. And even if some part of the worker found peace in death, it was not his body. Since cremation was not allowed in Durban, corpses had to be buried by the laborers at a location near a butchery designated for the burial of Indians and Africans. Workers at times did not bury the corpses deep enough, and the bodies were then sought out and eaten by pigs that had acquired a taste for flesh from offal thrown out by the butchery. "Not even in death was their dignity." Coolies were regarded as units of labor rather than human beings and this mentality made them susceptible to all forms of abuse. An editorial in the *Natal Witness* aptly sums up the attitude of the White colonists:

32. Ibid., 223.

> The ordinary coolie . . . and his family cannot be admitted into close fellowship and union with our families. He is introduced for the same reason as mules might be introduced from Montevideo, oxen from Madagascar or sugar machinery from Glasgow. The object for which he is brought is to supply labor and that alone. He is not one of us, he is in every respect an alien; he only comes to perform a certain amount of work, and return to India.[33]

Apartheid and Afrikanerdom

Before 1948, there were no pretenses that the National Party's laws served the interest of Whites only. Prior governments openly stated their intention to serve and protect the interests of Whites, particularly White economics, which could only be achieved by the exploitation of Black labor. It slowly dawned upon the Afrikaners that political domination by the Blacks would threaten White interests, and social segregation became the new goal. In 1940, Hendrik Verwoerd, who became known as the "architect of apartheid," refined and systematized the policy with the attempt to justify race segregation as an ideological principle that served both the interests of Whites and Blacks.[34]

By 1663, Afrikaners had segregated schools; by 1678 the prohibition of miscegenation carried with it the punishment of up to three years imprisonment with hard labor on Robben Island; a place where, centuries later, Nelson Mandela and other political activists spent most of their youthful years as political prisoners. By 1685, prohibition of marriages between Whites and Blacks became law. The first act of apartheid was Van Riebeeck's 1860 planting of the bitter almond hedge that drew the lines of separation and division. He gave the native people a derogatory name and took their land, their livelihood, their dignity, and their right to free movement. By doing so, he embedded the concept of apartheid deeply in Afrikaner nationalism.

In 1948, when the Afrikaner-dominated Nationalist Party swept into power for the first time under a platform of "apartheid" or "separate developments," previous trends of White policy were legally carried to their full conclusion. The plan was to close the remaining loopholes

---

33. Ibid., 224.
34. Kendall and Louw, *After Apartheid*, 31–32.

and secure an agenda that previous regimes had already initiated. The Nationalist government found new and arbitrary powers to administer programs that enforced restrictions on Black freedom and which promulgated a more elaborate ideology to the separate and unequal policy.[35]

Apartheid, "this insane policy," as Nelson Mandela called it,[36] was diametrically opposed to the most basic concepts of human rights. With the exception of Hitler's policy toward the Jews, nowhere did such an ideology exist that was legislated on a national level under the pretenses of a Biblical mandate. The Afrikaners believed themselves chosen by God to rule, and they had the vocal support of the Dutch Reformed Church. Enforced removals, unemployment, police abuse, and other inhumane treatment geared toward the Blacks sparked off riots, with the worst being in Durban in 1949. A violent quarrel between a young Zulu and an Indian provided an excuse for a crowd of Blacks to turn their suppressed rage at their hopelessness, oppression, and poverty toward the Indians, whom they resented as traders, foreigners, and exploiters.[37]

The Afrikaner's built Apartheid on the foundations of biblically cast narratives of the Great Trek and the Battle at Blood River, narratives which assigned self-serving destinies to each racial group with territorial separation as a foundational principle and then attributed it to the will of God. In God's name, then, they advocated homelands and reserves for each group. Blacks were prohibited from buying or residing on land outside the native reserves designated to them. These reserves were strategically located away from urban parts of the country, away from White areas, and away from mainstream resources commonly available to Whites. The only problem was that Whites needed Black labor on their farms and in the urban industrial areas outside the reserves.

This resulted in the provisions for "migrant workers" or "provisional sojourners," who were forbidden to be in the cities once their contracts were fulfilled or their labor was no longer required. It was understood that the city was a White area in which there was no place for an unnecessary "native" (another common term which referred to

---

35. Fredrickson, *White Supremacy,* 241.
36. Benson, *Nelson,* 35.
37. Ibid., 35–36.

Blacks). The Urban Areas Act of 1923 was an attempt to monitor the influx of Blacks into the cities. The Act divided South Africa into prescribed urban and non-prescribed rural areas, and strictly controlled the movement of Black males between the two. According to this act, Blacks entering the city were required to have jobs or were granted a limited time to look for work. Male workers were discouraged from bringing their families along to the cities because provided housing was in "locations" or "compounds" that could be controlled.

To enforce the "influx controls" Blacks were required to carry passes, indicating their current employment status. The Pass Law Act No. 67 of 1952 forced Black people to carry identification with them at all times. A pass included a photograph, details of place of origin, employment record, tax payments, and encounters with the police. It was a criminal offence to be unable to produce a pass when required to do so by the police. No Black person could leave a rural area for an urban one without a permit from the local authorities. On arrival in an urban area a permit to seek work had to be obtained within 72 hours. The South African police devoted a considerable amount of their time checking what became commonly referred to as a "pass book" which verified one's name, age, tribe, place of birth, a record of one's tax payments, employment details, encounters with the police and lawful area of residence. Failure to produce this document resulted in being loaded onto a *Kwela Kwela*, (a Zulu slang for a police pick-up van which literally meant, "to get on it") and transported to an uncertain fate which included being sent back to their reservations, imprisonment, subjection to forced agricultural labor, or removal to remote camps or villages to await the government decision on their livelihood.[38] The following story from M. Friedman's *I Will Still Be Moved*, illustrates the significance of pass books:

> Sadika lived in relative comfort with his wife and two children for thirty years and was registered as self-employed with the Labor Bureau in Johannesburg until he lost his Reference Book. He made application for a duplicate document and was given a temporary permit and was asked to return on a future date. When he did return, he was told that apart from the ten shillings he paid for the temporary permit, he had to pay an extra five shillings. Sadika protested. He was then told that if he

---

38. Ibid., 240–44.

refused to pay the extra five shillings he would be sent to the forced farming district. Upon hearing this, Sadika agreed to pay the extra five shillings only to hear that it was already "too late" and was taken to the Nigel Farm Labor Bureau. On the farm he was treated as a prisoner, guarded by African "overseers" known as "boss boys." Beatings took place regularly during the day. At night they were locked up in a filthy shack-like barn with dirty floors. A 44-gallon drum was cut in half and served as the workers' lavatory. These drums were brought in at night and removed in the mornings except for Sundays when the tins remained until Monday mornings. Needless to say, the place stank. Water was served in the same way, in one 44-gallon drum from which they were allowed to drink only twice a day, morning and evening. Due to the ration of water, it was common that the laborers would faint in the hot, blistering sun. When they lay unconscious on the ground, it was not uncommon under the command of the boss that the "boss boys" would urinate into the mouths of those unconscious, inviting others to do the same as an attempt to revive them. At other times, those that were unconscious would be beaten by the boss who accused them for faking because they did not want to work. Many died during these severe beatings and were buried on the farm.[39]

In 1950 the ban on interracial marriages was made law. This ban was an amendment to the Immorality Act, No. 21 of 1927 banning sexual relations between Blacks and Whites. It is ironic to note that one of the first documented violations of this ban was of a Dutch Reformed Church minister who was caught with a domestic worker in a garage built by his parishioners. Many Afrikaners satisfied their urges for sexual relations with Blacks by crossing the border to Swaziland, Lesotho, and Botswana.

The next piece of the apartheid puzzle was defining who belonged to what race. The Population Registration Act, No. 30 of 1950 was devised to define race based on physical appearance. A national register was created in which every person's race was recorded and a Race Classification board determined what a person's race was in disputed cases. The carrying of identity cards defining the race of a person became mandatory. The South African police used the "pencil in the hair" test to resolve doubtful classifications. If a pencil pushed in a person's hair stayed, this signified frizzy hair which then classified the person to

---

39. Paraphrase of Friedman, *I Will*, 62–69.

be either "Colored" (a term still used to define the offspring's of Black and White relations) or Black. If the pencil fell out, the classification was either "Colored" or White. This test, however, resulted in predictably inaccurate classifications with traumatic repercussions-often the splitting of families, evictions of people from their homes, and dismissal of children from schools.[40]

The next pillar of apartheid was the Group Areas Act, No. 41 of 1950. The intention was to restrict groups to their own residential areas of the cities and thereby to control trading and purchase of land in specified areas. The act forced physical separation between races by creating different residential areas for different races. This led to forced removals of people living in "wrong" areas. For example, in 1965 over 60,000 people were uprooted from their homes in District Six, Cape Town when the area was declared a "whites-only" zone. They were relocated to the bleak plains of the Cape Flats several miles away. Similarly, Sophiatown in Johannesburg was bulldozed to the ground in 1957 to make way for the "white area" of Triomf (meaning "triumph" in Afrikaans). The apartheid government was intent on enforcing "separate development" for different ethnic groups.[41]

The Group Areas Act had a significant impact on the Indian population. The attitude of the South African government toward Indians has always been, "Let them go back to India." In 1948, when the National Party came into power, the Prime Minister, speaking of the Indians said, "[T]hey are a portion of the population that does not belong to South Africa. When they have any grievance, they do not go to their own Government. Under the circumstances, they must be content to live in this country under restrictions."[42] Indians were not represented in Parliament and they could not enter White facilities. They attended segregated schools. They were also required to carry travel documents if they desired to travel from one province to another. Since the passing of the Group Areas Act, they were also victims of institutionalized robbery because on the grounds of their skin color, they were deprived homes and businesses that they acquired lawfully, with the savings and labor of many years.

---

40. Oakes and Steyn, *Illustrated*, 376.
41. See "Recalling District Six."
42. Friedman, *I Will*, 17.

Nana Sita, a 64-year old Indian man came as a trader to Pretoria in 1913. He started a business in 1918 and acquired a house attached to the business. Under the newly instated Group Areas Act, Nana Sita's business and house was zoned in a "White" area and he was forced to move. He was sentenced to three months imprisonment when he refused. His business and residence was later bombed. Imprisonment and violence seemed to be the solution to remove people who defied the laws of the government.[43]

The Separate Amenities Act established separate facilities such as toilets, washrooms, public transportation, post offices, offices, beaches, parks, bus stops, park benches, service counters, and elevators for Whites and "non-Whites." Justice Minister Charles Swart justified the purpose of the Act with the statement, "We will always find that reasonable amenities are provided for all classes according to their aptitude, according to their standard of civilization and according to their need."[44] P. W. Botha who later became State President argued in support of this act that in order to gain a clear view regarding fair treatment and the rights of non-Europeans, one should first answer the question, "Do we stand for the domination and supremacy of the European or not?" For if one stands for the domination and supremacy of the European, then everything one does must be in the first place calculated to ensure that domination.[45]

In the above section I have worked to give the reader a picture of the structural abuses of apartheid, abuses justified in Christian-inspired narratives, narratives that only benefited one group to which the Churches were subsequently compelled to respond.

The Role of the Church in its Struggle against Apartheid: The Assertion of Alternative Christian Narratives

The debate regarding apartheid and the churches' rejection of its un-Christian policies has a long history. Ever since apartheid became a policy in 1948, churches in South Africa have voiced strong objections to this dehumanizing policy. It is, however, far beyond the scope of

43. Ibid., 17–18.
44. Oakes and Steyn, *Illustrated History*, 377.
45. Ibid., 376.

this chapter to write on every event or conference that articulated or voiced the opinions of the Church. However, as the discussion of such events is necessary, I have therefore selected various significant historic statements that document the church's struggle in its debate against apartheid.

The Christian Council o f South Africa held a conference at the University of Fort Hare in 1942. This was an important year for those involved in the struggle against Hitler. The the purpose of the conference was to discuss the task of the churches in "Christian Reconstruction." A mood of optimism seemed to prevail among the conferees. Seven years later, the Christian Council convened again at Rosettenville, near Johannesburg. This time, the theme of the conference was "The Christian Citizen in a Multi-Racial Society." The mood of optimism that buoyed the conferees at Fort Hare was long gone and apprehension had taken root with the specter of apartheid.

The Rosettenville Conference was held in 1949, a year after the enactment of the policy of apartheid. This was the first ecumenical conference since the National Party came into power. Out of this conference, six fundamental truths were affirmed:

1. God has created all men in His image. Consequently, beyond all differences remains the essential unity.
2. Individuals who have progressed from a primitive social structure to one more advanced should share in the responsibilities and rights of their new status.
3. The real need of South Africa is not "Apartheid" but "Eendrag" (i.e. unity through teamwork).
4. Citizenship involves participation in responsible government. The franchise should be accorded to all capable of exercising it.
5. Every child should have the opportunity of receiving the best education that the community can give, and for which the child has the capacity.
6. Every man has the right to work in that sphere in which he can make the best use of his abilities for the common good.[46]

Even at this early stage with just a year after the National Party coming into power, Eendrag was still another possible narrative for some in

---

46. de Gruchy, *The Church*, 53–56.

the Afrikaner church. This could have been a brilliant opportunity for the church to change the National Party's heart from the narrative of segregation to togetherness; from discrimination to unity; from racism to equality. However, the church was governed by the NP and was there to support its policies and not make policy for government.

In 1952, Catholic Bishops issued a statement on race relations emphasizing the evils of discrimination on the basis of color and the inevitable results that follow from this type of thinking. Their statement maintained that "non-Europeans" (i.e. non-Whites) had a right to justice and a right to full participation in the cultural, economic, and political life of the country. The document went further in defining the basic principle of apartheid, which was the preservation of White civilization as White supremacy. This meant that only Whites ensured full political, social, cultural, and economic rights under the law. People of other races were to be satisfied with what Whites conceded to them, with the imperative not to endanger White privileges. This was absolute White supremacy, which overrode all possible justice and violated Christ's teachings. In 1957, Catholic Bishops formally rejected apartheid as fundamentally and intrinsically evil.[47]

In contrast, proponents of apartheid described the policy as allowing separate development, in which the different races were all given an opportunity to pursue their respective and distinctive social evolutions. It was maintained by the White race that this was the only way that all races would be doing the will of God and fulfilling God's providential designs. This may sound very noble but its practical implications were that Whites designated themselves agents of God's will, interpreters of God's providence, and determiners of the boundaries of non-White development. One trembles at the blasphemy of thus attributing to God the offenses against charity and justice that are apartheid's necessary accompaniment.

Although the 1952 bishops' statement acknowledged that segregation continued in the church, societies, schools, seminaries, convents, hospitals, and the social life of people, it concluded that the practice of segregation was officially not recognized in the Catholic Church and that in the light of Christ's teachings such practices could not be tolerated. The document exhorted White Catholics to pursue a change of

---

47. de Gruchy and Villa-Vincencio, *Apartheid*, 144–46.

heart and to practice the law that Christ demands. To all South Africans, an earnest plea was directed to carefully consider the true meaning of apartheid, namely that it is evil and anti-Christian, it arouses bitterness and resentment, and reduces contact between the various groups to an inhuman and unnatural minimum.[48]

The Dutch Reformed Church (known as the Nederduitse Gereformeerde Kerk) became involved in Africa when the Dutch settled in the Cape of Good Hope. It was only in 1824 that they formed their own synod in the Cape. After 1910 other synods were established around South Africa. Before 1857 the Cape synods indicated that the church ignored racial differences and wanted the church to be one for both Whites and Blacks. A separate church was not foreseen when in 1881 the Dutch Reformed Mission Church (DRMC) was formed to provide cohesion.[49]

The DRC has always had a great deal of influence in South Africa, since the it is integrally related with the Afrikaner nation, culture, and rise to power. It should not be assumed that all Afrikaners were or are members of the DRC, but it was quite clear that the DRC had significant influence on the policy makers of the nation. Most of members of Parliament and provincial councils were high ranking members in the church. The majority of the people employed by the government to fulfill various roles in institutions, including the military, police, and public office, were members of the DRC. The DRC has held tight reins and a considerable influence in the Black "daughter" churches. Based on its position in society and the influence it held both at the national and local level, it could be argued that the DRC held the keys to the future of South Africa.[50]

It is necessary to mention at this point that the relationship between the DRC and the English-speaking churches has been always plagued by misrepresentation and misunderstanding. It is also important to mention that criticisms directed towards the DRC could be equally applied to many other churches, but the DRC was usually an easier target because its position was always stated very boldly and because it had such strong influence in the country. All of the DRC's statements began

---

48. Ibid., 146–48.
49. Kinghorn, *Christianity Amidst Aparthei*, 57–59.
50. de Gruchy, *The Church*, 69–70.

with a principle taken from Scripture. Scripture was the ultimate test of opinions and actions.

The question becomes then how did the DRC interpret scripture. The DRC did not build its biblical basis for race relations with Old Testament passages such as Gen 9:25, "the curse of Ham," nor did it attempt to identify Israel with the Afrikaner. Instead, they made a great deal out of the creation narratives of Genesis 1–11. Out of their hermeneutic, two dominant narratives arose: 1) Scripture upheld the essential unity of humankind thus supporting the fundamental equality of all people; and 2) ethnic diversity was in accordance with the will of God. Thus, the Afrikaner saw Babel not only as a consequence of sin, but also God's preserving mercy.

The DRC brought these principles to an interesting conclusion. They maintained that while unity of humankind is a basic reality in creation, there is a distinction in creation that cannot be overcome in this world. Because the human race has been deeply marred due to human sin and unity has been seriously affected, the only hope for renewal and unity must come by God's redeeming grace through Christ. Thus, they believed that the ultimate restoration of unity would only take place at the final coming of the kingdom of God. In the mean time, the church must avoid the modern tendency to erase all distinctions among peoples. The DRC maintained that in serving human relationships, the church must regard justice as a basic concept, along with love, peace, and truth. The simultaneous principles of unity and diversity were also developed on the basis of the New Testament passages, which provide regulations on the basis of separate development and the co-existence of various races in the same country. Ultimately, then, the DRC rejected racial injustice and discrimination in principle, but at the same time accepted the policy of separate development.[51]

This appears to be a major contradiction, since separate development and apartheid are synonymous. However, it explains how the DRC's statements against racism were by no means an attack on government policy. For the DRC, the policy of separate development was not seen as a contradiction of Scripture, but rather that Scripture gave credence to the idea of diversity and supported the policy.

---

51. Ibid., 71–73.

In March of 1960, the country was horribly shaken by the dramatic events at Sharpeville where sixty-nine Blacks (mainly women and children), were shot and killed by the South African police. This event was precipitated by the protests of Blacks on the discriminatory pass laws and signaled the beginning of the Church's struggle against apartheid. In response to Sharpeville, the World Council of Churches (WCC), arranged a consultation conference with the leadership of the world's eight major Reformed bodies on "Christian race relations and social problems in South Africa," in December 1960.[52]

The WCC meeting took place in a suburb of Johannesburg called Cottesloe. The significance of this meeting was the presence of ten delegates each from eight South African member churches, one observer from the Christian Council of South Africa, and six delegates from the World Council of Churches. Among these 87 participants were seventeen Blacks and one woman. There were also representatives from the Nederduitse Hervormed Kerk (NHK, a division of the DRC which kept strong ties to the Reformed Church in the Netherlands), whose delegates were all White and kept to themselves. The NHK delegates were in frequent consultation with political leaders, including the Prime Minister. The conference was held behind closed doors and the concluding statement was comprised of three parts. Part one rejected all unjust discrimination, while supporting various opinions on apartheid. Part two addressed the need for consultation between all race groups on matters that affected them. Part three provided specific resolutions on justice in trials, the position of the Indian community in South Africa, freedom of worship on a multiracial basis, freedom to preach the gospel, and methods of future consultation and co-operation between the various South African churches.[53]

Needless to say, the conservative NHK rejected all the resolutions, most of which surprisingly, were prepared by the DRC delegation who also recommended that Coloreds should be enfranchised, a proposal which became very volatile and embarrassing for the government, since it was suggested by theologians of their own church.

The resolutions prepared by the DRC delegates and theologians drew a dramatic response from various sectors within the DRC church

---

52. de Gruchy and Villa-Vincencio, *Resistance and Hope*, 15.
53. For a detailed report of the consultation see Hewson, *Cottesloe Consultation*.

membership and from Prime Minister Verwoerd, who expressed his personal disappointment with the actions of the DRC delegation. Within a short period of time, the DRC fell into line with the government and rejected the role played by their very own delegation. The DRC rejected not only the resolutions that were drawn up by the WCC at the Cottesloe Conference, but also they rejected the convictions expressed by their very own theologians and trusted leaders. Subsequently, the DRC withdrew from the WCC.[54]

The DRC General Synod published a second and definitive statement called "Human Relations and the South African Scene in Light of Scripture" in 1974. This statement also seemed to search the scriptures for counter-narratives. The pronouncement of the synod began with a statement of principle based on the Scriptures, as did all DRC documents. The final paragraph of the 1974 report concludes,

> The Dutch Reformed Church is only too well aware of the serious problems in respect of inter-people, inter-racial and inter-human relationships in South Africa. It seeks to achieve the same ideals of social justice, human rights and self-determination for peoples and individuals, based on God's word, as do other Christian churches . . . If the Dutch Reformed Church does differ from other churches, the difference is not due to a different view of moral concepts and values or of Christian ethics, but to a different view of the situation in South Africa and the teachings of God's Word in this regard. There is no difference in ideals and objectives, but merely disagreement on the best methods of achieving these ideals.[55]

It is difficult to comprehend how two groups of people working with the same source and with the same concerns for justice and peace generated diametrically opposite solutions. It is apparent that the hidden agenda of the Afrikaner was self-preservation and protection of the Afrikaner community at large. The future of the Afrikaner people was heavily dependent on the success of the separate development policy. Instead of a melting pot or pluralistic approach, which would embrace ethnic differences in the formation of a national identity, ethnic separation was repeatedly stressed and, more importantly, underscored by theological language. According to the DRC, all of this was done to

---

54. de Gruchy, *The Church*, 66–68.
55. Ibid., 73–74.

eradicate racial friction and racial discrimination. Separationist policies were structured under the guises of what was called *petty apartheid*, which were small but unfair laws such as the prevention of inter-racial marriages, and *grand apartheid*, which implied the distinction of where Africans and Afrikaners could live, either in the townships or in the suburbs. This distinction allowed the DRC to assume the responsibility of insuring that separationist policies were implemented in a just manner.

What did separate development promise? The policy was said to help Blacks regain and strengthen their identities. Two questions arose: 1) Why must Whites determine whether Blacks needed their identities regained? It should have been the prerogative of Blacks to determine for themselves as to whether or not they needed a consolidated identity; and 2) Is it necessary for a group to be removed from society and placed into the remotest parts of the land for "identity development" to take place?

If doubts remain about the true intention of separationist policies, one should consider the fact that 87% of the land was designated to Whites and 13% of the land designated to Blacks, although 87% of the population was Black. In light of this fact, there remains no doubt that the apartheid policy was clearly designed for safeguarding White privileges, interests, land, resources, and identity.[56]

Opposing Theological Narratives

When considering Afrikaner political theology, one must be reminded of the actions taken by the South African government against its "political" clergy. The basis of Afrikaner political theology is evident in the assertion below, taken from N. Diederichs's thesis on Nationalism, written while he was a professor of political philosophy at the Free State University:

> The highest ideal order, that nation-transcending territory where nations meet each other in a complementary way, cannot be seen other than in a religious light. In religion every human life, every nation discovers its grounding and meaning. Without a religious point of relationship and an ultimate object, the universe, the nation and the individual would be

---

56. Ibid., 78.

incomprehensible, senseless, and purposeless ... On every particular nation especially there rests this special task to accept its providential role as a nation, and by realizing it to play its part in the ultimate attainment of the godly purpose of the universe.[57]

Although the Cottesloe Conference in 1961 is significant in that it was the last time both Afrikaner churches and mission churches met to consider the status of the South African context and what their role were, essentially it represented a White perspective. What could have been a place for dialogue and understanding for the NHK delegation turned out to be a group of anguished White clergy listening politely to their minority Black colleagues. It seemed obvious that the NHK delegation was convinced that a policy of differentiation could be defended from the Christian point of view. And, although while the DRC delegation rejected apartheid in principle, they continued holding steadfast to their Christian paternalism and patronizing ideologies.

The statement issued from the Cottesloe Conference regarding the racial problem, however, certainly caused controversy. It read:

> It is our conviction that the right to own land wherever he is domiciled and to participate in the government of his country is part of the dignity of the adult man, and for this reason a policy which permanently denies to the economically integrated non-White people the right of collaboration in the government of the country of which they are the citizens cannot be justified.[58]

The DRC spokespersons who collaborated with the National Party's policies had unilaterally inserted the phrase "economically integrated" because the insertion of the phrase would have the result of excluding all non-Whites (e.g. migrant laborers) from the polity they were creating. Most non-Whites were not "economically integrated." Even though they worked for Whites, they still belonged to the reservations and homelands. This phrase was excluded in the final version of the document. Upon seeing that it was excluded in the final printing, the DRC reacted strongly to the anti-apartheid tone of the document. They rejected the Cottesloe statement, withdrew membership from the WCC, and took action against two of their own DRC theologians who participated in crafting the statement, namely A. S. Geyser and Beyers

---

57. Mbali, *The Churches and Racism*, 42.
58. Walshe, *Church Versus State in South Africa*, 13.

Naudé.⁵⁹ Beyers Naudé, a Dutch Reformed minister, was a central figure in the Afrikaner cultural revival as a pioneer in promoting the Afrikaans language and as one of the founders of the Broederbond, the Afrikaner secret society. Naudé followed the family tradition, studying at Stellenbosch University, the center of Afrikaner thought, where he received degrees in language and theology in 1939. During that year he became the youngest member of the Broederbond and was ordained in the Dutch Reformed Church (DRC). For 20 years he was a pastor at various places throughout the country; among Afrikaners he served as a respected clergyman who was convinced of apartheid's biblical basis. His last position was in a wealthy Pretoria church attended by several cabinet members.

In 1960, Naudé was profoundly shaken by the Sharpeville massacre. Deeply disillusioned, he began an intense study of the Bible, searching the scriptures for a new biblically-based narrative, and concluded that apartheid was unjust and unsupported by the scriptures. Naudé had become acting moderator of his church district and then moderator, the highest local office. He directed the DRC to accept the final statement that rejected apartheid. In opposition, the South African Prime Minister, Hendrik Verwoerd, led a conservative backlash that repudiated the position and that resulted in the resignation of the DRC from the WCC. Naudé refused to alter his position in the face of the church synod's fury. In 1963 he resigned as moderator and founded the Christian Institute (CI), an ecumenical organization to pursue reconciliation through interfaith dialogue. For this action he was defrocked, and he subsequently left the Broederbond. Both Naudé and the CI were harassed from the start by the South African security forces. When invited to address a DRC youth meeting, he was dragged from the building by

59. Mbali, *The Churches*, 43. Beyers Naude, an Afrikaner, has been profoundly influenced by his associations and involvement with ecumenical work as one of the key figures in planning the Cottesloe conference together with other DRC theologians and the WCC. He tried to work both to reassess the policy of apartheid within Afrikanerdom and to work ecumenically for race relations, a tough role to play within the Afrikaner group. Under incredible pressure from the Afrikaners and the DRC, he was forced to resign from the secret Afrikaner organization called the Broederbond (Brotherhood). In August of 1963, he formed the Christian Institute. With dwindling support from the DRC clergy and membership, he was asked to choose between the DRC and the Christian Institute. He chose the Christian Institute. The DRC and the South African government had always been very successful in preventing voices from the margins, even from their very own tradition, as experienced by Beyers Naude himself.

DRC officials. Naudé spoke out against the rising tide of Black violence as well as against apartheid, but as CI became more radical, it allied itself with the liberation theology of Steve Biko's Black consciousness movement, which rejected both White racism and liberal paternalism. Many CI staff were banned or had their passports withdrawn.

Naudé and the CI began a process of sowing and raising up alternative Christian narratives among the churches. From 1977 to 1984, the South African government declared him a "banned person," which meant a de facto form of house arrest, that severely restricted his movements and interactions with others. In 1980 he resigned from the DRC and was received by the African Reformed Church, which accepted his ordination and gave him a pulpit. He succeeded Desmond Tutu as secretary-general of the South African Council of churches in 1984 and held this post until his retirement in 1987. Although he was never connected to the African National Congress, Naudé was named to its negotiating team for the 1992 constitutional talks with the government of F. W. De Klerk.[60]

The recommendations of the Cottesloe conference would not have been rejected by the DRC had it not been under pressure from the South African government. Acceptance of the recommendations would constitute rejection of the biblical and theological narratives underpinning apartheid. Prime Minister Verwoerd magisterially set the DRC theologians and delegates straight by convincing them that the WCC and their liberal views had strategically manipulated them. He reminded them that theologians too, had to have a single mind in affirming the high purposes of apartheid and he convinced them that they needed to recant their acceptance of the recommendations of the conference. It was Beyers Naudé who refused to change his decision. The night before the synod made its decision on the Cottesloe Statement he noted:

> I had to decide. Would I because of pressure, political pressure and other pressures which were being exercised, give in and accept, or would I stand by my convictions, which over a period of years had become rooted in me as firm and holy Christian convictions? I decided on the latter course, and put it clearly to the synod that with all the respect which I have for the highest assembly of my church, in obedience to God and my conscience, I could not see my way clear to giving way on a single one of

60. Gastrow, *Who's Who*, 153–54.

those resolutions, because I was convinced that those resolutions were in accordance with the truth of the gospel.[61]

Beyers Naudé, an Afrikaner cleric who spent half his life using the Bible to justify apartheid before becoming one of the anti-apartheid movement's most important moral voices died at a retirement village in Johannesburg, September 17, 2004. He was 89.

South African theology is essential in this process of alternative Christian discourses. It was, in fact, potent enough to shatter the stranglehold of Afrikaner interpretations of the Christian tradition within the public sphere and in public discourse. In addition, it also stands as a testament to the pervasive role theology has played and continues to play in political discussions within the South African context, the religious sanctioning of conflicting socio-political and economic interests of the European colonists since the seventeenth century, and the ambivalent, yet significant role the church has played and continued to play for and against the apartheid policies.

The majority of South Africans claim some form of Christian allegiance, however as previous testimonies reveal, this does not imply that all arrive at the same understanding of the practical implications of the teachings of Scripture. Since ones faith is often critically interwoven with one's personal interests, interpretation of Scripture will always be based on ones social reality and may be radically different from the interpretation of others. In this manner, the conflict between race and class in South Africa both influences and is influenced by theology.[62]

The impact of Latin American liberation theology and Black theology in South Africa has introduced a new methodology of doing theology in context. But most importantly, it stood as a testament to the possibility of a radically inclusive Christian narrative. Theological conflict as de Gruchy emphasizes, is a clash between worldviews, ideologies, and their related interests. One is bound to find theological conflict in societies where justice, power, and reconciliation are prominent issues and conflicting perspectives are being justified by "the will of God." Therefore, faith, theology, and politics have an inseparable relationship.[63]

---

61. As quoted in de Gruchy and Villa-Vincencio, *Resistance and Hope*, 9.
62. Ibid., 85.
63. Villa-Vincencio, *Between Christ*, 85–88.

This theological conflict of South Africa is closely linked to and in many ways a result of a biblically based origin myth, as discussed at length in the first half of this chapter. The first missionaries to arrive in South Africa were the Moravians from Hernnhut in 1737. They established a mission station among the Khoisan in the Cape. The self-supporting missionaries established enclosed settlements where "heathen" indigenous Africans could learn skills. They converted the African from one form of lifestyle to another with the intention that these converts would remain permanently in these new established communities. This model became a common feature in South African missionary work. Missionaries, in some regard, whether they were aware or not, served as agents working for the interests of the British imperialists.[64]

Majeke describes the role of missionaries:

> a remorseless process of peaceful penetration, who first approached the chief humbly, Bible in hand, and asked for a small piece of land to set up his mission station. At his heel hastens the trader, the purveyor of cheap goods…In due course follows an agreement on land between the chief and the governor, and the invaded tribes are split asunder, divide and rule. Under the capable hands of the missionaries carries on its deadly work of disruption. Throughout this period the missionaries are at hand preparing the way and disarming the chiefs with their message of God's peace. They make easy the negotiations between governor and the chief; they act as the governor's advisors and assist in drawing up the terms of the treaties. They become interpreters and peacemakers, while at the same time they are military advisors to the invaders.[65]

Scholars seem to have varied reactions to the missionary endeavors in South Africa. Those scholars who assume the settlers' viewpoint believe that missionary endeavors undermined colonialism by threatening the settlers' social and material interests. In contrast, others regarded the work of missionaries as crucial to European colonization, thus enforcing political and cultural domination. As with other topics in South African history, both groups justified their positions through narrative. Either way, it still posed a threat to African culture and their worldview. This discussion could be seen as the beginnings of both the

---

64. Boesak, *God's Wrathful Children*, 24.
65. Mareke, *The Role of the Missionaries*, 5–7.

"status quo theology" which served the interests of the settlers and their descendants in the struggle for power, and those missionary theologies that were intended to be in "support of Black interests." European theology imposed onto South Africans may have also created the way for the development of South African Black Theology, since the African Independent Church movement was born as a result of the DRC giving its support to the status quo and struggles of the Afrikaner.

When, in 1986, some DRC theologians made the bold discursive move of declaring apartheid a heresy, distinctions between evangelicals and ecumenists emerged in stark relief. Evangelicals stressed truth to the gospel while ecumenicals focused on unity of the church. Out of this rose the liberation movement, from traditional forms of theology through the advent of Black theology. Black theology, as a new Christian narrative in the South African context, was a response to Black consciousness among Black radical students in an attempt to enable Blacks to maintain their Christian faith on one hand while also discovering what Scripture had to provide as support to their struggle against apartheid. Black theology has learned from Latin American theologies, that "doing theology" in context cannot be separated from social analysis and praxis. The issues concerning Black theology are not only race, but also class. The struggle is not just between Whites and Blacks, but also between the rich and the poor, the oppressor and the oppressed. Black struggle cannot separate racism and economic exploitation.[66]

Theologian Lebamang Sedidi clarifies this inseparable connection of racism and economic exploitation in Black Theology:

> As long as the Black people in this country suffer a double bondage, racial oppression and economic exploitation, the task of Black Theology will always be double-pronged. Racial capitalism is the name of the game. That is the sin that Black Theology wants to uncover and eradicate in God's name.[67]

---

66. Villa-Vincencio, *Between Christ*, 88–94.
67. Sebidi, *A Critical Analysi*, 44.

According to activist and martyr Steve Biko,

> Black Consciousness is in essence the realization by the Black man of the need to rally together with his brothers around the cause of their oppression—the Blackness of their skin—and to operate as a group in order to rid themselves of the shackles that bind them to perpetual servitude.[68]

From an early age Steve Biko showed an interest in anti-apartheid politics. After being expelled from his first school, Lovedale, in the Eastern Cape for "anti-establishment" behavior, he was transferred to a Roman Catholic boarding school in Natal. From there he enrolled as a student at the University of Natal Medical School (the Black section). Whilst at medical school Biko became involved with the National Union of South African Students (NUSAS), but the union was dominated by White liberals and failed to represent the needs of Black students. Biko resigned in 1969 and founded the South African Students' Organization (SASO). SASO was involved in providing legal aid and medical clinics, as well as helping to develop cottage industries for disadvantaged Black communities.

In 1972 Biko was one of the founders of the Black Peoples Convention (BPC) working on social upliftment projects around Durban. The BPC effectively brought together roughly 70 different Black consciousness groups and associations, such as the South African Student's Movement (SASM), the National Association of Youth Organizations (NAYO), and the Black Workers Project (BWP) which supported Black workers whose unions were not recognized under the apartheid regime. Biko was elected as the first president of the BPC and was promptly expelled from medical school. He started working full time for the Black Community Program (BCP) in Durban which he also helped found.

In 1973 Steve Biko was banned by the apartheid government. Under the "ban" Biko was restricted to his hometown of Kings William's Town in the Eastern Cape—he could no longer support the BCP in Durban, but was able to continue working for the BCP—he helped set up the Zimele Trust Fund which assisted political prisoners and their families. Biko was detained and interrogated four times between August 1975 and September 1977 under apartheid era anti-terrorism legislation

---

68. Biko, *I Write What Like*, 49.

that allowed for indefinite detention without trial. On August 21, 1977 Biko was detained by the Eastern Cape security police and held in Port Elizabeth. From the Walmer police cells he was taken for interrogation at the security police headquarters. On September 7, Biko sustained a head injury during interrogation, after which he acted strangely and was uncooperative. The doctors who examined him (naked, lying on a mat and manacled to a metal grille) initially disregarded overt signs of neurological injury. By September 11th, Biko had slipped into a continual, semi-conscious state and the police physician recommended a transfer to a hospital. Biko was, however, transported 1200 km to Pretoria—a 12-hour journey, which he made lying naked in the back of a Land Rover. A few hours later, on September 12, alone and still naked, lying on the floor of a cell in the Pretoria Central Prison, Biko died from brain damage.

The South African Minister of Justice, James Kruger initially suggested Biko had died of a hunger strike. The hunger strike story was dropped after local and international media pressure. It was revealed in the inquest that Biko had died of brain damage, but the magistrate failed to find anyone responsible, ruling that Biko had died as a result of injuries sustained during a scuffle with security police whilst in detention. The brutal circumstances of Biko's death caused a worldwide outcry and he became a martyr and symbol of Black resistance to the oppressive apartheid regime. As a result, the South African government banned a number of individuals and organizations, especially those Black consciousness groups closely associated with Biko. The United Nations Security Council responded by finally imposing an arms embargo against South Africa.[69]

The Black consciousness movement strove to bridge the gap between ethnic divisions within the Black community, bringing together Blacks, Coloreds, and Indians who rejected separate development. The movement encompassed strong religious elements, with Christianity being its main emphasis. It was this movement that provoked theologians to question their theological insights and forced them to relate their faith to Black self-awareness. Black theologian Manus Buthelezi writes that "the evolution of the Black consciousness called for the need

---

69. For more on the story of Biko and other victims of apartheid see especially Truth and Reconciliation Commission of South Africa, *Truth and Reconciliation Commission of South Africa Report*, 1999.

to relate the Christian faith to the experience of the Black man."⁷⁰ It is also true that Black theology conversely provided the theological foundation for the Black consciousness movement as Ernest Baartman expresses:

> No more is he (the Black man) going to try and fit into a non-White portrait drawn by the White man. No more is he going to say what the White man wants to hear and thus continue his own indignity. No more does the White man epitomize all that is good, just, and of, value . . . Black consciousness is the Black man saying "yes," he says yes to who he is in Jesus Christ.⁷¹

From a Community of Believers to a Community of Citizens

The church division in South Africa is a division caused by clashing Christian narratives. The Afrikaner church approached the South African situation by conforming to the status quo. The Cottesloe Consultation is a good example of this. On the other hand, the Pentecostal churches took a totally different approach to the situation. Theirs was one of denial and indifference based on the principle that spirituality is and should always be the main focus of the church. The problem with the Pentecostal perspective was the presumption that spirituality and politics should never be mixed. The Black and English-speaking churches seemed to be the only ones that took up the struggle to oppose the status quo. I hasten to add that not all English-speaking churches took this position. To this day, almost all churches are still divided across race lines with separate churches for Blacks, Indians, Coloreds, and Whites with pockets of integrated churches around the country. This is based on the premise of Apartheid and status quo theology that each race group should have its own church. Little communication existed between the various churches. There was little interaction between these churches, which resulted in unfamiliarity with each other's worlds, living conditions, social problems, needs, fears, and ambitions. Due to this unfamiliarity, the White Afrikaans-speaking churches had little knowledge of the circumstances and experiences of Black Christians. This was White

---

70. Kretzschmar, *The Voice of Black Theology*, 61–62.
71. As quoted in Ibid.

resistance to change at its best. Whites were convinced that change is not necessary due to lack of knowledge caused by church apartheid.[72]

President F. W. De Klerk's famous speech at the opening of Parliament early in February of 1990 marked the beginning of hope for Black South Africans. Hope that would start the country towards a new beginning; hope that would set the platform for a process of reconciliation among all people and change that would drastically alter the future of South Africa. Black South Africans were used to having their hopes and aspirations dashed by White political leaders who lacked the conviction to break the domination of White privilege and move toward a united people a new community, a new South Africa where all were recognized with full citizenship.[73]

President P. W. Botha was ousted from office by successor F. W. De Klerk in September 1989. During De Klerk's campaign he announced that the government intended to grant full citizenship to all South Africans, including Blacks. In an article of February 4, 1990, the *Sunday Times* printed the following:

> We awake on this summer, Sabbath morn in a country where hope has displaced fear, despair and anger. Where there is a feeling that South Africans may yet have a decent chance of making it. After decades of evading the truth ... A page of history has been turned and all of us, regardless of pigment or political persuasion, today confront a new future. It's Sunday; prayers are in order.[74]

Thus it is evident that even in an apparently public, secular media like the *Sunday Times*, interpretations of weighty events were still cloaked in religious language and biblical imagery.

---

72. Alberts and Chikane, *The Road to Rustenburg*, 63. *The Road to Rustenburg* is a collection of some of the most influential and well respected theologians in South Africa. The book is filled with perspectives on the role of the church as it looks forward to the future, the new South Africa. The present reference is to an address, "The South African Reality," presented at this conference by DRC theologian and professor, Koos Vorster.

73. Cameron-Dow, *The Miracle*, 8–9. The *Sunday Times* is a national newspaper in S.A. The referenced work here is a collection of newspaper articles from 1990–1994. It includes all the significant events that made headlines in South Africa, from the release of Nelson Mandela to the momentous event when all races in South Africa were given the right to vote.

74. Ibid., 13.

In this very same year, President De Klerk appealed to the South African church leaders to formulate a strategy conducive to negotiation, reconciliation and change. In a country where state Christianity had become synonymous with the Verwoerdian philosophy of "separate development," the President's invitation rekindled feelings of animosity, which would have made his association with the initiative untenable. While some believed that De Klerk's request emanated from sincere Christian conviction, others viewed it as political manipulation, and still other saw it as gesture to satisfy the international community. Ironically, in the dusty little town at the heart of ultra right-wing Afrikaner territory, the historical Rustenburg Declaration of November 1990 employed theological language to condemn apartheid, and unequivocally proclaimed that apartheid was sin.

This declaration was the result of a National Conference of churches in South Africa. Two hundred and thirty delegates, including guests from overseas, representing ninety-seven denominations and forty organizations, participated in the Rustenberg Conference, which later became known as the "Road to Rustenburg." The goal of the conference was to work towards a united Christian witness in a changing South Africa. The conference was unique in many aspects because it covered a wide theological spectrum (from Catholics, to Calvinists, to Pentecostals), as well as different political, cultural and business spheres. It brought together the Dutch Reformed Church, Pentecostals, and Evangelicals.

A surprising event took place at the conference when Dutch Reformed theologian Willie Jonker, confessed and asked forgiveness for his own, and his Church's, complicity with a system that promoted and supported racial discrimination. Reaction to his confession among Black Christians varied from cynicism by some, especially the Black Reformed Church, to complete acceptance by Archbishop Desmond Tutu. On a more significant note, this event of recognition and articulation of injustice set a precedent that would cause the event to go down in history as "The Conference of Confessions." Many in churches of South Africa responded, repented of the past, and set a new course for the future.[75]

---

75. Alberts and Chikane, *The Road*, 13–16.

Former President P. W. Botha, upon hearing of the events at the conference was angered by the DRC's public confession. It infuriated him that the church that supported the policy of apartheid recanted and deemed it sinful and heretical. President Botha declared that he found it

> utterly unacceptable that the DRC theologian had confessed to Archbishop Tutu. It is beyond my comprehension that they could have done something like that. If anyone needs to do some confessing, it is Tutu himself. With his continuing sanctions mongering and support for revolutionary elements, he has caused untold suffering and misery to many women and children.[76]

Viewpoints differed at the conference, with Evangelicals and Pentecostals emphasizing evangelism as the answer to the South African problem and the solution for a new dispensation and The South African Council of churches stressing the need for social justice. However, mutual recognition for each other's views nevertheless promoted harmony and a sense of unity. Although opinions differed, it became clear that the Church played a significant role in developing the new South Africa, by acting as a conscience to the state and requiring the establishment of a just political system.[77]

The Apostolic Faith Mission of South Africa— Past, Present, and Future

I would like to draw this sketch of South African narratives to a close by exploring one of various examples of counter-narratives, which show the intimate relationship between struggle and discourse. American missionaries, John G. Lake and Thomas Hersmalhalch, started the Apostolic Faith Mission (AFM), the largest and the oldest Pentecostal denomination in South Africa in May 1908. From its inception, the AFM emphasized the supernatural power of the Holy Spirit, with speaking in tongues as the main evidence of being "filled in the Spirit." It has a strong missionary zeal and is well established in various African countries. The AFM started as a non-racial church. Early attempts to introduce racial separation in worship were resisted by the founding

---

76. Nelson, *The Miracle*, 39.
77. Alberts and Chikane, *The Road*, 16.

missionaries. However, when the missionaries left the country to return to their homelands, the church was set on a course of racial separation in compliance with the racial ideology of the country. Protests by the Blacks were not heeded, because a paternalistic mentality characterized the White churches' involvement with regards to the Black church.[78]

The White church had its own executive committee and president elected by Whites. The executive committee appointed a mission director who took responsibility for what was called "daughter" churches, or "mission" churches. These daughter churches were the so-called African, Colored, and Indian congregations. The mission director chaired all the meetings of these churches. These churches were merely extensions of the mother church, i.e. the White church, the true church. The mission church was just a stepchild.[79]

As the political environment changed in the country, the AFM also began to question the racial divisions in the church in relation to the Gospel. As a result, starting in 1975, the issue of unity began to appear on the agenda of the church councils of the four sections of the church. However, these talks were still through the missions department of the White church, making them bilateral talks between the three sections of the church and the White church. No progress was made until 1981 when the Colored division of the church adopted radical resolutions demanding unity. The threat of the church breaking apart renewed unity talks, which assumed a collective form with representatives of the various sections negotiating together. A sequence of events followed which led to the adoption of an important document in March 1986, called the "Declaration of Intent" on unity based on biblical principles. The document rejected apartheid and racial discrimination as unbiblical. This document became the basis for further negotiations on the unity of the church.

Five years of unity talks and discussions followed, which varied between hope, despair and frustration on both sides. No discernable positive results toward unity were achieved. A crisis point was reached in 1991, which led the three mission churches (African, Coloreds, and Indian) to unite without the White section in May 1992. The union of the mission churches revitalized negotiations between the White and

---

78. Apostolic Faith Mission Church Pamphlet, *88 Years of Grace*, 1–3.
79. Chikane, *No Life of My Own*, 20.

Black churches. In June 1992, a new constitution was agreed upon between Whites and Blacks, which took into consideration the existence of the two divisions. For the first time in the history of this church, the Constitution set the two divisions on an equal footing. The White church was referred to as the "single" division, and the Black church as the "composite" division. In May 1993, the new leadership of the Composite division elected Frank Chikane as President.[80]

After 21 years of intense and painful negotiations continued between the two divisions, an agreement on structural unity of the church was first established. The composite division adopted the draft of a unity constitution in July 1994, and the single division adopted it in April 1995. On April 3, 1996, the AFM became the first church in South Africa to unite all races together and to constitute the united church on the basis of a mutually agreed upon constitution. The AFM set the precedent, moved towards community, pointed to a way of transforming the South African society from a racially and ethnically divided society to a society that is based on the values of Christian faith, and began the process of healing the pain and wounds of separation caused by the policy of apartheid.

Conclusion

In this chapter I presented a historical study of a complex country whose different ethnicities had been in conflict. These conflicts culminated in the rise and crisis of apartheid. The narrative of a community of believers struggling to make sense of faith was explored. The

---

80. Pamphlet, 2. Frank Chikane has played a key role in the political process of South Africa. As an ordained minister of the AFM, he had been imprisoned several times by the S.A. Government for his involvement in politics. During one of his incarcerations, he was removed from his congregation. Since he was imprisoned for his political convictions, he was regarded as a terrorist by the White church. This was precisely the strategy of the apartheid system. They would detain legitimate leaders of the community for representing the grievances of their communities and thereby criminalize them. This was how they justified brutal and inhuman acts against Blacks to stop them from resisting oppression and exploitation. In 1982, Chikane was suspended as minister of the AFM due to his involvement in politics. Chikane was the first Pentecostal to be the secretary of the South African Council of churches, a position he held until 1993. He played a key role in steering the committee for the National Conference of churches in S.A. in 1990. Chikane was elected as chief advisor to the Mandela administration early in 1996 and is currently Chief Advisor to President Thaba Mbeki, and serves as Vice President of the AFM under the new constitution and unity of the church.

narrative focused on the struggle for power, land and political dominance between the indigenous peoples of South Africa and the Afrikaner. I demonstrated how the Afrikaner's conviction that they were the chosen people proceeded along a path of maintaining the *volk* and "choseness" through the laws of apartheid and the support of these laws through scripture and the Dutch Reformed Church. An autonomous force moving through history, worked its way through the Apostolic Faith Mission Church to bring unity and healing within the denomination as a symbolic and prophetic gesture to set the stage for what was to be experienced by all South Africans four years later in 1994.

According to Martin Luther King, Jr. racism, poverty, and war are the greatest barriers to human community.[81] It seems in 1990 the future of South Africa that President Mandela envisioned was no different from the America that King struggled to achieve in the sixties. Like King, President Mandela had a firm and clear vision of a multi-racial democratic society, a vision that reflected the values of democracy. King dreamed of a democratic, egalitarian society as a beloved community. Mandela dreamed of a society of individuals who viewed themselves as independent aspects of one whole, realizing their fullest life where communal contentment was the absolute measure of values.

South Africa is viewed today as a great example of how a society can move beyond the bondage of racial and tribal factionalism to assume a non-racial and egalitarian posture. President Mandela insists that South Africa will teach the world how true democracy should function. He declares,

> I personally believe that here in South Africa, with all our diversities of color and race we will show the world a new pattern for democracy ... I think that there is a challenge to us in South Africa to set a new example for the world.[82]

Creating multicultural institutions is an important element in a pluralistic society that works toward community. Racial walls need to be broken down. Behavioral scientists Jackson Bailey and Evangelina Hovino suggest that, "Multicultural organizations need to:

---

81. See Baldwin, *Toward the Beloved Community*, 144.
82. Cited in Baldwin, *Toward the Beloved Community*, 169.

- Reflect the contributions and interests of diverse cultural and social groups in its missions, operations, and product or service,
- Act on a commitment to eradicate social oppression in all forms within the organization,
- Include the members of diverse cultural and social groups as full participants, especially in decisions that shape the organization, and
- Follow through on broader external social responsibilities, including support of efforts to eliminate all forms of social oppression and to educate others in multicultural perspectives."[83]

The struggle for democracy and equality has a long history in South Africa. Community cannot be reached when groups of people consider themselves superior and others inferior or made less in the image of God. Nor can community be achieved when one race justifies their discriminatory actions Biblically at the expense of suffering and torture of another race. This is heresy, and must be confronted. This was the role of the Black church in South Africa. In an inclusive and interracial society, freedom and justice for all must be guaranteed. In 1990, the dismantling of apartheid, symbolized by the release of Nelson Mandela established the rule of Black majority. The barriers to human community crumbled and all ethnic and racial groups integrated their resources and talents to uplift the South African society in totality. While on the threshold of rebirth, South Africa still faces an unprecedented identity crisis, due to chasms that divide its people. Nelson Mandela could be seen as a symbol of community and reconciliation. A community that transcends all artificial human barriers and in which the chains of conformity do not shackle the individual remains a pertinent goal for the South African community in the years ahead.

The church in a new emerging reality is to be responsible in the transition to democracy. It is to overcome the bitter legacy of apartheid. The church is to be politically and socially involved but must also sustain its vital character of liturgical life and personal piety. It must take an active posture in helping rid people of fear, deception, hatred, greed, and negative attitudes, which prevent authentic community. The challenge of the more unified South African church is to keep hope alive as only certain elements of it did so effectively during apartheid.

83. Bailey and Hovino, "Developing Multicultural Organization," 14.

It has an obligation to empower spirituality and morality for the kind of transformation that results in reconciliation, nation building, patriotic cooperation, and genuine interpersonal and interracial community living.

2

Deconstructing Oppressive Narratives
The Case of Co-opting Paul

Introduction

DUE TO THE AFRIKANERS' CONVICTION THAT THEY HAD A COVENANTAL destiny as the chosen race to carry out God's plans and purposes for the future of South Africa, they leaned on the Bible for guidance and direction. Romans 13 would be an important text to support the Afrikaners' view of covenantal destiny as a mandate to rule South Africa unswervingly and faithfully. In this chapter I explore Romans 13:1–4 with an intentional purpose to access other possible contexts in which Paul may have written this letter. This is not the classic traditional reading of Romans 13 but rather an alternative reading as a case of co-opting Paul to deconstruct South Africa's oppressive meta-narrative. My conclusion is a far removal from the traditional interpretation of this text and does not intend to undermine or lessen the traditional interpretation. However, I believe this chapter will provide an alternative perspective to Romans 13 that is both supported by the biblical text and important for the present exploration of the South African narrative.

Since this has been the determining passage in the New Testament for the political ethic of church-state dialogue, it is important to portray its original meaning as carefully as possible. First, my study will consider the textual authenticity of the passage; second I will examine the passage in the context of the letter and the social make-up of the church in Rome; third, I will explore Paul's teaching as outlined in this passage; and fourth, I will discuss how the Afrikaner Church in South Africa utilized this passage to support apartheid.

Paul Minear's frustrated confession demonstrates his struggle with this pericope. "I must admit," he states, "that I am unable to find particular reasons in the Roman situation for Paul's inclusion of this teaching . . . concerning obedience to the governing authorities."[1] But, such scholarly frustrations are not necessarily comforting to those like Martin Luther King, Jr., Alexander Solzhenitsyn, Dom Helder Camara, or the Japanese-Americans stripped of their rights, loyalty, and dignity during World War II. What are Christians imprisoned for their faith in Uganda, South Korea, and the Philippines to make of these words? What about Paul himself, regularly beaten and jailed for insisting on proclaiming a new gospel of authority? And Jesus? And Stephen? Is it possible that Paul was referring in Romans 13 to those governments of his own time that he so thoroughly denounced in 1 Corinthians 2?[2]

The Problem of Textual Authenticity

Scholars who have wrestled with the closing chapters of Romans have frequently discussed the exact relationship of Rom 13:1–4 to its epistolary context. Some, like James Kallas, have posited the view that the closing chapters show evidence of emendations and revisions. Chapter 16, for example, is said to have existed as a separate epistle. Kallas and other have advanced some of the strongest arguments in favor of Rom. 13:1–4 as an interpolation.[3] However, others who attest to the section as Pauline find it indifferently related to its setting. Ernst Käsemann believes that, although in many respects it is unique to Paul, "there is no reason to dispute the authenticity of the text" and concludes that this section is "an independent block."[4] Scholars have also attempted to show that it is not simply an intrusion into the context, but that it has significant ties to what precedes and follows.

Robert Stein, among others, provides some convincing arguments that the text flows smoothly out of 12:18–21, (see v. 18, "If possible, so far as it depends upon you, live peaceably with all.") since in 13:1–7, Paul is asking Christians to live peaceably with the state. Further, he notes Paul talks about the wrath and vengeance belonging to God in

---

1. Minear, *The Obedience*, 88.
2. Ogle, "What," 259.
3. Kallas, "Romans," 365.
4. Käsemann, *Commentary*, 350–52.

both 12:19 and 13:4–5. The word *apodote* (pay) in 13:7 is also found in 12:17, which leads Stein to conclude that the paying of the debts of taxes and tribute in 13:7 alludes to the "debt of love" in 13:8.[5]

In contrast, Hutchinson refers to this pericope as an "erratic boulder" due to its lack of continuity between the passage and its context.[6] He believes that, "Do not be overcome by evil; but overcome evil with good," (12:21) has its proper sequel in "Let no debt remain outstanding, except the continuing debt to love one another, for he who loves his fellowman has fulfilled the law," (13:8). Hutchinson also notes the style of 13:1–7 does not fit with the immediate context. It is that of a diatribe and has an approach of Jewish Hellenistic Wisdom teaching. It appears that the play on words *hypotassesthō* and *antitassomenos*, and the repetitiveness of *gar*—seven times in these seven verses—and *agathos*—three times in two verses (vv. 3–4)—appeals to the reason or the *nous* of the reader. Furthermore, this passage is unlike the rest of Paul's writings, which are eschatological and Christologically focused. All these factors cause Hutchinson to doubt that the passage is Pauline.[7]

Cullman however, disagrees with Hutchinson's concern that this passage is not eschatological. He maintains that this passage is set, "in a context of clear expectation of the end," and thus he argues, "Paul's view of the state is that it is a temporary institution, nothing final or absolute, God makes use of the State as long as this age endures."[8] By taking this perspective, Cullman further supports Pauline authorship and the continuity of this passage with its context.

In contrast to the aforementioned supporters of Pauline authorship, Kallas gives two general and three specific reasons for concluding that this section is an interpolation. His first general observation revolves around the fact that ch. 16 "once existed as a separate epistle," since scholarship has revealed that texts from the second century ended the epistle at 14:23. The four closing benedictions, 15:13, 33; 16:24, 27, provide ample evidence for him that there must have been "some type of confusion or reworking" of the closing chapters. His second general

---

5. Stein, "The Argument of Romans," 325–26.

6. Hutchinson, "The Political Implications," 50.

7. Ibid.

8. Hutchinson, "The Political Implications," 51. However, Hutchinson feels that "Cullman's observation does not merely heighten the incongruity between the passage and the eschatological setting into which it has been obtruded."

observation is that "nowhere else in any of Paul's epistles does he ever discuss the state and the Christian's relationship to it." This strikes an "alien note" since it is a foreign subject.[9]

Kallas' first specific rationale for viewing this pericope as an interpolation is supported by the fact that theologians have always recognized this to be a "self-contained envelope completely independent of its context." For example, Kallas quotes Morrison, who claims it "does not seem to have any logical reason for being there, and any special reason for Paul's directing this exhortation to Rome is not immediately apparent."[10] Also, Kallas, in support of the passage's independence, notes the various monographs written on this section without reference to the sections preceding or following.

Second, Kallas sees this independent block as an interruption to the context, maintaining that ch. 12 and 13:8–14 would flow more smoothly if it were not for this intrusive section. By drawing connections to various parts of Mathew Kallas points out the intrusive nature of this passage. Paul, in ch. 12, seems to be echoing Jesus' Sermon on the Mount. "Present your body as a living sacrifice," (v. 1) is associated with Jesus' call to deny one's self and take up the cross (Matt 16:24). Likewise, Matthew 5:2–12, 39, and Luke 6:27 seem to be reproduced by Paul in 12:14–21. Romans 13:8–10 is grammatically similar to Matt 5:21, 27, and Rom 13:19b is identical to Matt 22:39b. Kallas sees this as "synoptic-type teachings." Therefore, he concludes that this intrusive envelope does not belong here, and disrupts the flow of Chapters 12 and 13.[11]

Third, Kallas notes how these verses contradict some of the basic Pauline ideas and forms of expressions. In Paul's writings, the "end of the world" is a constant, as evidenced in his Thessalonian epistles, the first letter to the church in Corinth, and the epistle to the Romans. Kallas appeals to the words of Schweitzer to support this view of Paul: "From the

9. Kallas, "Romans XIII," 365.

10. Ibid. Kallas quotes Morrison: "This passage lacks specific syntactical connection with what precedes . . . Any reason for Paul's directing this exhortation to Rome is not immediately apparent." See Morrison, *The Powers*, 104. Barrett too remarks about the abrupt break and new beginning of this section: "The new paragraph, a self-contained treatment of a special theme, appears first to be introduced somewhat abruptly." However, he does not see this section as an interpolation. See Barrett, *Commentary*, 244.

11. Ibid., 366.

first letter to the last Paul's thought is always uniformly dominated by the expectation of the immediate return of Jesus."[12] However, an immediate return of Christ does not seem to be the view of the author of the interpolation, who assumes the continuation of the world indefinitely and attempts to define the relationship between the Christian and the state, with a "statement of loyalty to the ruling authorities."[13]

Another example of Pauline particularities is that Paul always speaks of "governing authorities," or "rulers of this age" with reference to cosmic rulers or supernatural figures, but the reference here indicates human figures. Both Morrison and Barrett support Kallas' view that the usage of *exousia* elsewhere is always in reference to spiritual powers.[14] Paul saw "principalities" and "powers," not as flesh and blood, nor as servants of God for the service of civilian affairs. However, the author of this section sees the powers as human servants of God, loyal to that task. In the "eschatological-demonological" worldview, Rome was not seen as a benefactor or as an instrument for the service of God, but rather as a tyrant. Therefore, it is inconceivable that Paul would speak of Rome in an exalted manner. If the passage is Pauline then one wonders if Paul is being both hypocritical—this is not how he speaks of the authorities elsewhere—and servile— he exalts them to a position they really do not deserve. If this is the case, then he is being inconsistent with his own theology. Ultimately Kallas concludes that the only solution to this textual inconsistency is to assume that this section was written after Paul, when the failure of the world to end forced the church to re-evaluate its relationship to the state.

Kallas' view is convincing and very appealing for our present discussion. I agree that 13:1–7 could be seen as an interruption in the epistle and that the text as a whole would flow more smoothly if it were not for this intrusion. However, I will show that this pericope is neither an intrusion nor an interpolation. Using Marcus Borg's alternative exegesis and Mark Nanos's treatment of the Jewish context of Paul's letter,

---

12. Ibid., 367.

13. Ibid., 368.

14. See Ibid., 365–69. Kallas notes that Morrison points out, "Sound New Testament scholarship can affirm the consistency of exousia with a meaning different from Paul's usual meaning, but it also uses the word in isolation-something which Paul nowhere else does." (368) Kallas also notes Barrett recognition that this passage lacks the usual Pauline references to "spiritual-angelic powers, demonic authorities." (368)

I will show that this passage is not intended to provide principles on the Christians' relationship to civil authorities, but is intended to be interpreted within the context of Jewish nationalism.

In response to Kallas' argument that the ending of the epistle has been altered radically, it must be said that while there is continuing discussion about the authenticity of ch. 16 and parts of ch. 15, it is not a foregone conclusion that they are falsified. Therefore, one cannot conclude that the text in question, which is deep within the paraenetic section of 12:1—15:13, is compromised by the questionable nature of ch. 16. The problem of ch. 16 cannot be assumed to have occurred again in 13:1-4. Stein's arguments that the text in question is connected and flows smoothly out of ch. 12 should be equally considered. So, what then are we to do with this text? In my opinion, textual authenticity of this independent block does not invalidate the paraenesis found here, especially since historically this has been a significant text for Christian political ethics. Therefore, serious attention needs to be given to the context, interpretation, and teachings of this passage.

Romans 13:1–4 in Context

Since the apostle is addressing the church in the capital city of the empire, according to Morris, it would be "suitable to say something to them about the role of the State."[15] There were Jews who objected to acknowledging a heathen king by paying taxes in support of a heathen state. Furthermore, Morris proposes that there could have been restive Jews in Rome akin to the Palestinian Zealots who recognized God as the only King and rejected taxation by any heathen king.[16] If this were the case Paul may have wanted to caution the Roman Jews from taking any revolutionary stance toward the state.

Although Käsemann does not dismiss the idea that "Paul is calling enthusiasts back within the limits of earthly order," (based on the Corinthian experience and the introduction in 12:3), he considers it unlikely that there were any rebellious tendencies among the Jewish Christians.[17] Since they enjoyed the privileges of a recognized religion,

---

15. Morris, *The Epistle*, 458.
16. Ibid. "cf. the Rioting about 'Chrestus' of which Suetonius wrote and Claudius's expulsion of the Jews from that city, Acts 18:2."
17. Käsemann, *Commentary*, 350.

he concludes that the Jewish expulsion under Claudius had only "local causes and consequences," and is doubtful whether many Christians were involved.[18] He is much more inclined toward the idea that among the Jewish Christians, there were many who placed a greater emphasis on heavenly citizenship and consequently treated earthly authorities and rulers with animosity and indifference. Käsemann believes that Paul directed the exhortation of Rom 13:1–7 to Jews with this particular attitude.[19]

William Herzog presents three proposals for the specificity of this address. The first proposal uses Käsemann's argument "that Paul wrote to dampen the excesses of enthusiastic elements in the Roman church community."[20] Käsemann maintains that enthusiasts wanted freedom from human structures, and did not want to pay taxes. Paul responds to these enthusiasts by asserting "the role and place of the state in the provisional order of things."[21] Several scholars, however, critique Käsemann's argument. For example, Elliott notes that Käsemann's category of "enthusiasm" was so vague, and the "social phenomenon so unsubstantiated for Rome," that he had to rely on the Corinthian correspondence to describe "enthusiasm" in Rome.[22] McDonald agrees with Elliott's critique that Käsemann is too dependent on the Corinthian correspondence. However, McDonald critiques Käsemann's evidence as not deriving from the inner logic of the passage itself, since there is little evidence in the Roman epistle of confrontation with charismatic excess.[23] Käsemann's argument is further weakened according to Dunn, if 13:6, "διὰ τοῦτο γὰρ καὶ φόρους τελεῖτε, is taken as an indicative, (this is also the reason you pay taxes) rather than an imperative, (for this reason, you must even pay taxes)."[24]

Borg's reading from "Suetonius about Claudius's expulsion of the Jews from Rome for the agitation over Chrestus," is the basis of Herzog's second proposal.[25] According to Borg's interpretation of the text, there is

18. Käsemann, *Commentary*, 350.
19. Morris, *The Epistle*, 351.
20. Herzog, "Dissembling," 351.
21. Ibid.
22. Elliott, *Liberating Paul*, 219.
23. McDonald, "Romans," 545.
24. Dunn, *Romans*, 766.
25. Herzog, "Dissemlbling," 352.

agitation engineered by messianic Jews, which if combined with Jewish nationalistic sentimental expressions, could lead to an open break with Rome. Hence, Paul asserts this caution on the importance of order and the futility of rebellion, and recommends submission of one's self to the authorities.[26] In response to this proposal, Elliott finds no reason to doubt that the Jews in Rome were sympathetic to the Judean nationalist struggle. However, he also finds no evidence indicating that "Paul sought to rein in anti-Roman agitation among the Jews in Rome."[27]

Herzog outlines a third proposal developed by Stuhlmacher, which argues that Paul's counsel to the Romans is to "pay their taxes and indirect tolls and imposts out of respect for the divinely ordained purpose of the state."[28] According to the reports of Tacitus, a grievance report was submitted to Caesar regarding the extortion practices of the tax and duty collectors. Caesar, in responding to the grievances, actually considered "relinquishing the paying of taxes altogether," but this was not followed through.[29] The report of Tacitus also notes that if the extortion continued and the greed of these tax collectors did not stop, then he would fear that this situation would prolong and escalate, possibly leading to a revolt against the Roman empire. Suetonis' biography of Nero confirms this situation. These extra-biblical sources indicate that at the time of composition of the Roman epistle, there was a stirring among people who suffered high taxes and duties throughout the Roman Empire. Stuhlmacher concludes, that the 13:1–7 section, "which appears to be formulated in an entirely different fashion, is in fact aimed in verses 6–7 at a Roman situation which is both contemporary and pressing."[30] Although this hypothesis is attractive to many interpreters, some have criticized it for the lack of explicit support found in the text itself.[31] Porter, among others, argues for the lack of historical evidence that taxation was even an issue and that there is no textual evidence that Paul was even aware of this situation at the time of his writing.[32]

26. Borg, "A New Context," 207.
27. Elliott, *Liberating Paul*, 219.
28. Herzog, "Dissembling," 352.
29. Stuhlmacher, *Paul's Letter*, 200.
30. Ibid., 200–1.
31. Elliott, *Liberating Paul*, 219.
32. Porter, "Romans," 116.

Paul's epistle to the Roman church is a continuation of the "synoptic words of Jesus," as cited in 12:14–21. When Jesus commands, "love your enemies," (Luke 5:27–29a, 32, 35a; Matt 5:39b, 44, and 46), the implication, according to Paul, is "love your enemies, the Romans." Hence, Jesus' sayings are not just "generalizations about passive non-resistance, but counsel to not join in armed resistance to Rome."[33] Therefore, "love your enemies" refers to "disavowal of a militant anti-Roman policy." Borg wonders,

> Is it possible . . . that Paul is telling the Roman church to avoid entanglement in an anti-Roman policy? If so then Romans 13:1–7 . . . would naturally be interpreted in the same context: do not attach yourselves to the militant policy advocated by certain Jewish groups, for the Roman government is God's minister of judgment at this particular point in history.[34]

In contrast to the previous arguments for context specificity of the passage, O'Neill believes that this section, "was incorporated into a larger ethical section, 12:1—15:15, at a very late stage, maybe even after that section was itself incorporated into Romans."[35] He argues that no reference was made to this section before 150 CE or even after 180 CE. He continues that this section is neither Christian nor Jewish in origin, since both traditions "commanded respect for earthly rulers, but never the absolute obedience laid down in this section."[36] His suggestion is that this section was comprised of eight points collected by a Stoic teacher, who held that everything that existed "was derivative from God and, in a derivative sense, was God . . . Rulers owed their power to God absolutely, and they had to be submitted to of necessity."[37]

O'Neill offers two possible reasons why this collection gained a foothold in the Christian setting. The first was that it was simply material circumstance, because it agreed with the Jewish-Christian tradition, which believed in the divine source of earthly ruling powers and supported their authority to collect taxes and expect obedience. Secondly, O'Neill proposes that the collection was brought into the Christian

---

33. Borg, "A New Context," 207.
34. Ibid., 207–8.
35. O'Neill, *Paul's Letter*, 207.
36. Ibid., 208.
37. Ibid.

setting purely by accident because 13:8 agreed with the last sentence of the Stoic collection.

For O'Neill then, the reason for the incorporation of this collection is that the later Church needed some direction and guidance in relating to the State. This material, simply by circumstance, fitted that need and was incorporated into the text.[38] O'Neill's "accidental circumstance" is speculative and difficult to accept. The fact that the Stoic collection was in agreement with v. 7 ("give everyone what they are owed,") and v. 8 ("Owe nothing to anyone,") is too coincidental to provide sufficient proof against Pauline authorship. However, O'Neill does add support to the interpolation theories thereby increasing doubt about Pauline authorship.

We must ascertain more about the Jewish church in Rome. Did the Jews in Rome know about the chaos in the Palestinian homeland, and was there continuing contact between Palestine and Rome? Jerusalem was the geographic center of faith. Almost 50,000 Roman Jews, like Jews elsewhere, went on pilgrimages to Jerusalem to pay the temple tax. Delegations from Palestine to Rome were frequent; and, since Rome was the imperial capital, it was also the center for political, economic, and cultural traffic. We can assume that the Jews in Rome were aware of the events in Palestine.

We must also ask whether the Jews in Rome were subject to some of the same issues as the Jews in Palestine so that an anti-Roman sentiment may have existed among these groups. It is known that in 4 BCE, after the death of Herod the Great, "two events point to the sympathy of Roman Jews for Jewish nationalistic sentiments."[39] A delegation of fifty Palestinian Jews went to Rome to plead with Augustus for governance from Rome rather than leaving Palestine under the control of the Herods. Though the request may seem anti-nationalistic, it illuminates the Palestinian detest for non-Jewish kings and the Palestinian belief that the Sanhedrin could enjoy more autonomy under a Roman governor.[40]

38. Ibid., 208–9.
39. Borg, "A New Context," 209.
40. Ibid., 209–10. Borg writes, "Josephus himself uses the word, 'autonomy,' for a return of control of Jewish domestic life from the non-Jewish Herods to the Jewish senate." The Palestinian Jews "wanted independence; but if no independence was to be had, the next best thing was cultural home rule under a Sanhedrin of their own

In the same year, an impostor pretending to be Alexander (Herod's son by Mariamme) arrived in Rome to claim the Judean throne. The Jews welcomed him with enthusiasm. Why would Jews show enthusiasm for a son of Herod when his previous sons opposed the Jews in Rome? According to Josephus, Borg suggests, the real Alexander "had Hasmonean blood in his veins through his mother Mariamme . . . he was among the last of the Maccabees, whose memory was one pillar of Jewish nationalism."[41] Even apart from the sympathy of their compatriots in Palestine, the Jews in Rome had cause to distrust Rome. They suffered frequent abuse under Roman policies and general anti-Semitism in the Mediterranean world. They even suffered expulsion under Tiberius in 19 CE and Claudius in 49 CE. Therefore, the Jews in Rome probably shared the hope for a liberated Palestine, because it involved a sentiment of anti-Roman policy.

How did the church in Rome respond to this? Surely, this must have been of some concern to the Roman Christians, since many church members had association with Judaism. The Roman Christians would have asked what should be their attitude toward the anti-Roman sentiments of the Jewish Christian community. Borg's reading of Romans confirms for him that the Jewish Christian sentiment was a concern of the Roman church. Therefore, Israel is of particular emphasis in the epistle to the Romans, arguably more than any other Pauline epistle.[42]

With this in mind, Elliott concludes that the text in question "not only fits into its immediate context, but that it also has an intimate connection to Romans as a whole. The connection lies in the question of the Roman church's obligation to Israel."[43] However this may increase our understanding of the historical context into which Romans was written. Elliott finds no satisfactory explanation as to "why Paul would respond to this specific situation with just this argument."[44] Considering the two possible issues over taxation and military rebellion against Rome, the question is whether suggesting that the magistrates are there to serve

choosing-autonomy that would grant them their own religious traditions. Such autonomy was unthinkable under a Herodian prince. It was quite conceivable however, under a Roman governor." See also Simkhovitch, *Toward*, 12–25.

41. Ibid., 210.
42. Ibid., 210–13.
43. Ibid., 214.
44. Elliott, *Liberating Paul*, 219.

the good and punish the bad might change the minds of the Jewish Christian community.⁴⁵

This passage for Elliott, "stubbornly resists integration with the argument of the rest of the letter."⁴⁶ Elliott suggests that Borg is reading the theology of Romans through the lens of Ephesians. Dunn offers a different explanation, which has to do with the political realities confronting various Christian groups in Rome. Dunn agrees that the Gentile Christians ran a risk of "being identified with Jews in the wake of the Claudian expulsion."⁴⁷ Therefore, Paul writes to caution the church on being subordinate to the ruling authorities in order to avoid putting new congregations at risk. This explanation, once again, is not adequate for Elliott. Elliott proposes that these verses should be read as if they belong to this epistle, "as part of an argument addressed to a church in which the Gentile Christian's inclination to dispossess the Jew, politically as well as theologically, has provoked the apostle's concern."⁴⁸

Elliott's argument combined with factors of Borg's view (i.e. that Paul is concerned about the chasm that exists between the Gentile and Jewish Christians) is most agreeable among the several theories. However, for Borg, Jewish nationalism is the issue; for Elliott, the concern is Gentile Christianity. It seems possible, however, to posit that this Jewish nationalism festered into an anti-Roman sentiment, which may have caused a chasm between Gentile and Jewish Christians. Such a scenario could be the reason for Paul's admonishment to bridge the gap between Jews and their Jeiwsh nationalism as manifested in their anti-Roman sentiments. It was fine to be nationalistic but not at the expense of being separatist, which could lead to anti-demoscratic practices.

Mark Nanos contends that Paul's instructions were not concerned with the state, empire, or any secular organization but rather with the Gentile Christians responsibility and associations with the synagogue of Rome in their practice of the new faith. He maintains that it was not uncommon for Gentile Christians to attend synagogues; and therefore, Paul is instructing the Gentile Christians to subordinate themselves to the leaders of the synagogues. Further, Paul's instruction sheds new light

---

45. Ibid., 219–21.
46. Ibid., 220, contra Borg.
47. Noted in Ibid., 221.
48. Ibid., 221.

on the "stumbling" of non-Christian Jews as a witness of God's work. The "stubmling of some of the children of Israel was actually in the vicarious service of bringing the gospel to the gentiles, thus they are now indebted to love those stumbling as both brethren and neighbors and to live with those stumbling in harmony."[49] For the pericope in question, Nanos believes that Paul's address to "every person" (13:1) is a reference to Gentile Christians. The paraenetic material means to remind them of their new lifestyle wherein they are to conduct themselves responsibly and appropriately in the "congregation of the people of God to which they now belong as new members of the synagogues of Rome."[50]

In Yoder's treatment of this text, he criticizes positivistic and normative views that have commonly been presented by scholars.[51] In the positivistic view, the existence of governments is a virtue by act of institution by God. In other words the very act of government is a providential action of God in bringing it to being. The normative view holds that it is more the principle of proper government that is ordained and not particular governments. In other words if a government maintains certain standards such as good governments who care for the betterment of its people and nation then they can claim divine institution. Rather Yoder proposes that God does not create, institute, nor ordain governments but orders them and brings them into line as representing God's permissive governments. I find this lining up of permissive governments according to his purposes very discomforting since it is naïve to accept that power comes from God only when governments conduct themselves as rewarding and punishing evil. Nanos's idea that this text refers to synagogue relations of the Gentile Christians is as compelling as Borg's reading of the text that there must have been differing opinions between the Roman and the Jewish Christians with regard to "chosenness" and particularity of the gospel. The Jews considered themselves the chosen ones. Palestine, especially Jerusalem, was the center of faith, not Rome. This could support the theory that there were those among the Jewish Christians who were more concerned with heavenly citizenship and showed little regard to earthly rulers, since they bore no allegiance to Rome. There could also have been among Jewish Christians

---

49. Nanos, *The Mystery*, 291–92.
50. Ibid., 291 (see 291–95 for fuller discussion).
51. Yoder, *The Politics of Jesus*, 200–203.

those who believed that Gentile Christians were not truly part of the citizenship of the gospel.

This is similar to the South African Afrikaner who believed that they were the chosen race of South Africa, and the true citizenship of South Africa. Therefore, they had a special key to heavenly citizenship and the correct hermeneutic to interpret Scripture. According to the Afrikaner, it was as if all other races in South Africa were Gentile Christians, and not of the true citizenship of God. However, they were not the chosen race and, in fact, assumed the role of the Roman Empire legislating and establishing a theology to benefit their own interests. This theology was received with much speculation among the Gentile South Africans and resulted in a festering of anti-South African sentiments toward the state, similar to the anti-Roman sentiments of the Jewish Christians.

It is to this sort of context that this pericope speaks. Somewhere between Borg and Nanos, Paul's instruction was, "not intended as a generalized statement about the Christians' attitude toward all civil authority at all times, but a statement with a particular meaning to the Roman church for that particular situation."[52]

An Examination of the Text

According to Harold Dyck, Romans 13:1–7 could be summarized as follows:

> Be subject to the governing authorities and not to resist them, for they have been instituted by God. The ruler is, in fact, God's servant for their good, bearing the sword as an avenger to execute God's wrath on the wrongdoer. Those who do good need not fear but may expect approval. Conscience, not only fear of wrath, should motivate their subjection as the authorities attend to their service of God. Taxes, revenues, respect, and honor should, therefore, be rendered to those to whom they are due.[53]

Dyck exposes two apparent concerns Paul in the text: 1) to establish a right way of thinking about rulers in reference to their institution by God (v. 1), and their role as servants of God (vv. 4, 6); and 2) to promote

---

52. Borg, "A New Context," 215.
53. Dyck, "The Christian," 45.

a right relationship to rulers through his admonitions to be subject (vv. 1, 5) and to fulfill all proper obligations (v. 7).[54]

The word *hypotassomai*, ("to be subject, to submit," vv. 1, 5) is a hierarchical term, which stresses the relation of a person to his or her superiors. The meaning in classical Greek was "to place under." The subordination which *hypotassomai* connotes may be either voluntary or compulsory. Thus, it appears Paul is claiming that the Christian should voluntarily submit, in love, to divinely instituted authorities.[55] Several commentators note that the verb in the text, *hypotassesthō*, could be understood in the middle voice, thus meaning, "subject yourselves or submit yourselves."

Hutchinson challenges interpreters who find *hypotassesthō* to mean "obey." The New Testament typically uses *peitharcheō, peithomai*, and *hypakouō*, to mean obey. He notes that forms of *hypotassomai* are found 21 times in the LXX, and only once is the word used to connote the idea of obedience. Furthermore, it occurs thirty times in the New Testament, but the idea of obedience is not dominant. Thus, Hutchinson understands *hypotassomai* to mean recognizing civil authority, "as part of God's plan for the world but not blind uncritical obedience to that authority's every command," since Mark 12:17 indicates that there are limits to what is owed to Caesar.[56] Susan Boyer seems to agree with Hutchinson in finding the verb in vv. 1, 5 ambiguous. She prefers "subordination" as a better interpretation than "obedience," since the root, *-tasso* [set macron over o], means "to appoint, order, or to arrange." In light of an understanding of the word in Eph 5:21 as "reciprocal obligation," Boyer suggests that in Romans Paul is claiming "that one must do what needs to be done for maintenance of a just state."[57]

The Greek terms that are typically understood to refer to governing authorities are *exousia* ("authority, power," vv. 1–3) and *archontes* ("rulers," v. 3).[58] But, on must ask if these powers and rulers are spiritual or secular. Should the Christians in Rome submit to a governmental power and authority, or is Paul exhorting them to submit to some

---

54. Ibid.

55. This inference of voluntary submission to authority is rooted in Jewish wisdom traditions. See Hutchinson, "The Political," 54.

56. Hutchinson, "The Political," 53–54.

57. Boyer, "Exegesis," 209.

58. Neufeld, "Submission," 93.

sort of spiritual power? Cullman believes that the powers are angelic beings, which he links to the Jewish idea of a supernatural council of nations with a different angel representing each country.[59] Cullmann, amonng others, according to Abineo, associates the "rulers of this age" in 1 Cor 2:8 as invisible *exousiai* with their human instruments, Pilate and Herod.[60] According to Stein, Cullman's basis for this interpretation is that Paul's use of *exousia* elsewhere always refers to angelic powers. He rejects Cullman's interpretation for two reasons: 1) Paul never tells his readers anywhere else to submit to these angelic authorities; and 2) the context clearly demands that the primary meaning of this term must refer to governmental authorities to whom taxes and tribute can be given.[61]

Stein's rejection of Cullman's is sound. However, Ogle's argument that *exousia* is not a reference to governmental authorities offers an alternative to both Stein and Cullman. He proposes the following:

> Authority refers to the author of power, of relationships, of creation. Caesar, government, and the state do not create or author things or people. Rather, they manipulate, arrange, and redistribute others power and relationships ... exousia means of or from being, that which really is. For Jesus it is an understanding that God is transforming the world, re-authoring it so that humility, service, and love best expresses our living in God's authority.[62]

According to Ogle, Paul never uses the words, "government," "state," "nation," "empire," "Caesar," or "police" in this passage. Although "authorities," "tribute," and "sword" may refer to the state, they are also used in the New Testament to refer to God's word through the Holy Spirit among the people of God. Ogle concludes that "higher authority" (v. 1) would best suit this context if it were interpreted as the servant leadership of the church.

Since there are no compelling reasons to assume Paul is speaking of political authorities here, one might conclude the specific words indicate synagogue and/or church authorities. He begins by suggesting that

59. Cullman, *The State*, 93–114.
60. Abineno, "The State," 23.
61. Stein, "The Argument," 328.
62. Ogle, "What," 255.

every "soul" be subject (v. 1). After speaking of the redemption of "bodies" in 12:1, it is unlikely that he would request that souls be subject to the state. He adds a modifier to "authorities," *hyperexousais* ("higher"). Paul's only other uses of this rare word are the three occurrences in Philippians, where Paul refers to the peace of God (4:7), the knowledge of Christ (3:8), and the importance of imitating Christ's obedience of subordination and humility (2:3).[63] Furthermore, *hypotassō* is used thirty-eight times in the New Testament: nineteen times the word is refers to obedience to God; nine times to members of one's family or household; and six times to the church leadership in Jesus' name. There are four passages, including Rom 13: 1 and 5, which may suggest submission to political powers; however, the dominant use of this word is submission to God or to God's people.

Therefore, one may concur with Ogle's argument that the passage becomes consistent with its context if "higher authorities" is interpreted as servant-leadership of the church. Chapter 12 asks all Christians to be living sacrifices, enabling each other to love enemies. Chapter 13 shows the way to do it. Ogle's translation of the passage captures this understanding:

> Let every soul be subject to the higher authorities, for there is no genuine authority apart from God, and those continuing in God's ordination. So the ones resisting the authority have opposed God's direction, and, having opposed God's authority, will take judgment on themselves. For the church's servant-leaders are not a fear to the good work (e.g., feeding hungry enemies 12:21) but to the evil (e.g., executing your own style of justice in wrath 12:20 or lying to the Holy Spirit as Ananias and Sapphira did [Acts 5:1–11]). If you do not want to fear authority, do good and you will be praised for it.[64]

This is Paul's suggestion to the Roman church. In order for it to be accomplished, however, the members must submit to the church authorities, the servant-leaders, since the very role of church authorities is to enable them to establish harmony.

---

63. Ibid., 255–61.
64. Ibid., 260.

The Afrikaner Church and its use of Romans 13:1–4

The interpretation of Romans 13 has been important to Afrikaner theology in support of the oppressive governmental policies in South Africa. In this section I will show how the Dutch Reformed Church used Romans 13 to support its apartheid ideology. The following remarks illustrate the prominent use of Romans 13 in the South African socio-political context during the apartheid era. Theologian and activist, Allan Boesak relates the following story:

> On 19 October 1977, I was visited for the first time by the South African Security Police. They stayed from 3:30 a.m. till 7:00 a.m. At one point I was challenged by the Security Police who assured me that he was a Christian and, in fact, an elder of the White Dutch Reformed Church, on my persistent resistance to the government. "How can you do what you are doing," he asked, "while you know what Romans Thirteen says?" In the hour-long conversation that followed, I could not convince him. For him, as for millions of other Christians in South Africa and across the world, Romans 13 is an equivocal, unrelenting call for blind unquestioning obedience to the state.[65]

P. W. Botha, former State President of South Africa, addressed a gathering of a million members of the Zion Christian Church in April 1985, three months before a State of Emergency was announced:

> The Bible . . . has a message for the governments and governed of the world. Thus we read in Romans 13 that every person be subject to the governing authorities. There is no authority except from God. Rulers are not a terror to good conduct, but to bad conduct. Do what is good and you will receive the approval of the ruler. He is God's servant for your good.[66]

In 1974, the Dutch Reformed Church published a document called *Human Relations and the South African Scene in the Light of Scripture*. In section 49.1 entitled "Task of the Church," the document declares the Church must recognize that the state is an institution of God and have "competency in its own sphere." In this document, the church and the state are repeatedly reminded that the church must respect and "acknowledge the different character and competency of the authorities."

---

65. Botha, *Subject to Whose Authority*, 1.
66. Ibid.

It is neither the place nor the role of the church to dictate to the state on how "exactly they should regulate the intercourse and relationships between the various groups in a multinational situation. Because the Bible does not provide a clear indication on the nature of the structures by which the mutual relationships should be regulated."[67]

On the function of the state, the document declares that the state's duty was "to preserve public order within its own particular jurisdiction." It should act in accordance with Biblical norms, that is, with the love of God and neighbor as the guiding principle in the administration of justice. The state was empowered by Romans 13:4 to use power and the sword to keep the "pervasive influence of sin" in check. Finally, it declares that the state could not "degenerate into a totalitarian system in which the state usurps the sovereignty of other institutions . . . in order to regulate all aspects of human existence."[68]

In maintaining the heretical, inhuman policy of apartheid, the state usurped the sovereignty of all other institutions that protested against the apartheid policy and the evil it perpetuated in society. In actuality, the state reacted by banning those organizations, imprisoning their leaders, interrogating their families, banning all forms of peaceful marches, calling any gathering with more than five participants illegal, and calling for a permanent state of emergency from the early 1980s until 1990. Political prisoners were beaten and sometimes murdered while the state claimed "suicide" as the reason for their deaths. Such activity defines an authoritarian and totalitarian form of government that usurps the power and sovereignty of other institutions. Ironically, the DRC continued to support the state passionately contrary to its very own document.

On the conduct of church vis-à-vis state, the document states that the church is to submit to the state and its laws. "As far as its participation in the normal processes of justice and the exercising of its civil rights are concerned, provided the legal order does not conflict with the Word of God." The church is to hold the state accountable in accordance with the norms of the Bible, particularly in respect to relations with humanity and social justice. However, the church once again failed miserably in protecting civil rights. The church made a concerted

---

67. NGK, *Human Relations*, 2.
68. Ibid.

effort to assure that Whites were treated with special privileges and that justice was always preserved for Whites only. This behavior indicates either that the church believed that all non-Whites were not human, or that the church simply looked the other way when the concerns of Blacks were at issue.

On Human Rights, the document concludes with, "Rights and privileges may not be withheld when the claim is just." Clearly during apartheid Whites asserted their rights and privileges but Black request for justice was not considered valid and the church refused to acknowledge that Blacks had a right to justice. The whole struggle of the Black church has been a call for justice, yet the White Church did not acknowledge this. Once again this is a clear indication that the practitioners of the document catered only to the needs and privileges of Whites and that the church's beliefs existed only in principle and not in practice.[69]

In July 1985, President P.W. Botha declared a state of emergency to deal with the increase of violence in the Black townships. This action legalized detentions without trial and other previously illegal practices, supposedly so that the South African police and defense forces could uphold the laws mandated by the government. As a response to this, the Black church protested government's actions and called for a strike. Because of the state of emergency, 153 church leaders and theologians, Black and White, issued *The Kairos Document*, which was a theological critique of the South African situation.[70]

Beyers Naudé, one of the leaders who endorsed *The Kairos Document*, said it was intended to draw the attention of church leaders to a theological interpretation of the South African situation. The document addressed three types of theology:

1. State theology, which upheld the status quo of the state as seen in the theology of the DRC;

2. Church theology, which portrayed itself in colluding with the state in subtle ways by putting more emphasis on reconciliation than justice; and

---

69. Ibid.
70. See Kairos Theologians, *The Kairos Document*.

3. Prophetic theology, which purported that if a regime is tyrannical then it forfeits its moral right to govern and the people have the right to utilize ways to protect their interests against injustice and oppression.[71]

The document's chapter, "Challenge to Action," advocates,

> The church should not only pray for a change of government, it should also mobilize its members in every parish to begin to think and work and plan for a change of government in South Africa ... The Church will have to be involved at times in civil disobedience. A Church that takes its responsibilities seriously in these circumstances will sometimes have to confront and to disobey the State to obey God.[72]

The Kairos Document criticizes state theology as the "theological justification of the status quo with its racism, capitalism, and totalitarianism. It blesses injustice, canonizes the will of the powerful and reduces the poor to passivity, obedience, and apathy."[73] The question that arises is how state theology accomplished this. The Kairos Theologians attempt to answer this question by looking at four key principles found in state theology: 1) the use of Romans 13:1–4 as justification for imbuing absolute and divine authority to the state; 2) the idea that Law and Order determined control; 3) the use of propaganda toward whoever disagreed with state theology; and 4) how the name of God was used to support state and it practices.

---

71. Johnston, "Churches," 193. This article is an excellent synoptic analysis of the history, politics, churches' role and reconciliation movements in the struggle against apartheid. The article formed the ideas for the present chapter and it is recommended as a brief historical compendium for those who do not want to get bogged down with all the details of the South African situation.

72. Kairos Theologians, *The Kairos Document*, 30. *Kairos* is a Greek word that often designates a special moment of time when God visits his people to offer them a unique opportunity for repentance and conversion, for change and decisive action. It is a time for judgment. It is a moment of truth, a crisis (see for example, Mark 1:15; Luke 8;13; Rom 13:11–13; 1Cor 7:29; Titus 1:3; Rev 1:3). In June 1985, the crisis under apartheid intensified as more people were killed, maimed, imprisoned and the Black townships revolted against the racist regime. People no longer agreed to toe the line and cooperate with their oppressors. Fighting the fear of death daily as the apartheid army moved into townships to rule with their guns, theologians expressed the need to reflect on the situation, which resulted in this document.

73. Ibid., 3.

In response to *The Kairos Document*, F. P. Moller, an Afrikaner and President emeritus of the Apostolic Faith Mission Church, the largest Pentecostal denomination, asserted that Rom 13:1–4 provides one with the clearest biblical statement on government. He explained that its objective is to combat and destroy the power of evil and sin, while at the same time promoting good. Thus, it challenges the authorities to be servants of God. They must "endeavor to get evil people away from their wrong ways, to punish those that do wrong . . . rehabilitate them and even put to death those that do wrong . . . on the other hand they must provide protection and freedom for those that do good."[74] Moller suggested that the only norm for determining good from evil is the Word of God. The evil person is one who separates himself, his ideology, group, personal cravings, and aspirations from God and makes life decisions based on misguided desires. The government must act according to the norms of the "Bible and has divine authority on its side. Such an authority must be honored and obeyed."[75] Moller concludes that those that resist this authority must be punished.

While refusing to interpret the biblical texts in their appropriate context, state theologians assumed that Paul presented us with the absolute and definitive doctrine about the state. They too easily forget that Paul was addressing a particular community in Rome. Nowhere in the Bible does it require obedience to oppressive authorities. On the contrary, the Bible is replete with examples from Pharaoh to Pilate, who did not have a divine right to rule and oppress. God's will was that of freedom and liberation for the Israelites; Romans 13 certainly could not be contradicting this. The Roman Christians to whom Paul addressed his letter were not revolutionaries or people who tried to overthrow the government. They did not call for a change of government, nor was Paul addressing the issue of just or an unjust state.

The "authorities" to which Paul was referring in this text were church authorities, or church-servant leaders, and not the secular state. Some conservative approaches to biblical texts tend to support uncritically existing oppressive systems. Theologians of status quo or state theology misused Romans 13 by throwing it into the faces of those who raised objections against the beneficiaries of oppressive systems.

---

74. Moller, *Church and Politics*, 35.
75. Ibid., 36.

The text was used to maintain the status quo by making Christians feel guilty when they attempted to challenge the injustices in society brought about through the policies of an unjust government. Many proponents of overly conservative approaches to Scripture feel that they have no right to question Romans 13 or governments seemingly ordained by God in it. Romans 13 served well in maintaining the status of the beneficiaries, while those who were victims of society were just good students of missionaries with good intentions but were possessed with colonial ideologies. Romans 13, however, does not call for illogical obedience to evil systems. "It is racist missionaries, colonialists and theologians of the West . . . who developed this tradition to maintain Western domination and imperialism."[76]

The state manipulated the concept of law and order, to maintain the status quo. The state used Romans 13 to support their institutionalized oppressive policies of apartheid. Anyone who rejected this law and order was seen as lawless, and therefore guilty of sin. Establishing law and order is the duty of the state but there is no divine mandate to select the kind of law and order that is beneficial to one group of people at the expense and suffering of another group. Law and order are automatically moral and just simply because they have been instituted by the state. Proponents of state theology believe that the government had a God-given right to use violence to enforce an oppressive system of law and order. However, the law and order was instituted and enforced only to insure the status quo of oppression.[77]

Moller clearly supports this "state" view of law and order by adding that, when Paul speaks of earthly authorities in Romans 13, all people must submit since it is "not a power next to God but something instituted by Him and to whom it must be subject."[78] Where there is conflict between God and the state, God must be obeyed, but if one has to suffer, one must do so "with cheerfulness." This view does not give the option to "campaign for another form of government with other political, social, or economic systems." Moller asserts, "a weak, oppressive and unjust authority is still preferable to no authority where chaos reigns. However good or bad . . . just or unjust . . . oppressive or liberal . . . Autocratic or

---

76. Concerned Evangelicals, 28–29.
77. Kairos Theologians, 5–6.
78. Moller, *Church and Politics*, 37.

democratic," it is still to a greater or lesser degree resisting the power of evil, chaos, and destruction.[79]

Some forms of evangelical theology, with legalistic tendencies, accepted the apartheid system of law and order without questioning the nature of the laws they were supporting. Such law and order viewed Blacks as inferior and subhuman, not as men and women made in the image of God. It exploited Blacks and required them to submit peacefully to their oppressors and exploiters.[80]

The government viewed anybody that questioned state theology as communists. Opposition and rejection of state theology was said to have communist influences. The state used the name of God constantly to support their heretical theology. The preamble to the apartheid Constitution reads,

> In humble submission to almighty God, who controls the destinies of nations and the history of peoples who gathered our forebears together from many lands and gave them this their own; who has guided them from generation to generation; who has wondrously delivered them from dangers that beset them.[81]

It was presumptuous of this government to claim that the God of the Bible destined Whites from Europe to take possession of the land in South Africa. Their settling in South Africa had definite economic reasons. The god to whom they referred must have had strong negative feelings toward Blacks, since this god seemed to oppress Blacks and favor Whites. This god was the god of teargas, guns, beatings, prisons, and murders. To Christians, this god can be no other than the devil himself and the misuse of the name of God is nothing short of blasphemy.[82]

According to Moller, the theological unrest in South Africa is connected with Communism cloaked in religion, which is the result of Christians not being able to discern between true believers and false ones. Moller adds that in South Africa, communism has disguised itself in "liberation theology" or "contextual interpretation," which he claims "pretends to make the Bible relevant and practical for the South African

---

79. Ibid., 37–38.
80. Concerned Evangelicals, 31.
81. As found in Kairos Theologians, 7.
82. Concerned Evangelicals, 32.

circumstances."[83] From his perspective, liberation theology is actually the "camouflaged religious projections of Marxism and Communism."[84] Since this theology appears to be the champion against apartheid, "the political and economic unrest in South Africa" is the perfect context for this theology to breed.[85] Moller attempts to make his point by giving examples of documents that demonstrate communism and liberation theology: "the best known documents regarding liberation theology ... the Kairos Document, and portions found in the Evangelical Witness in S.A."[86]

Here lies the distinct difference between state theology and Black theology: anyone who spoke against state theology or spoke for Black theology was said to be communist. This type of propaganda infiltrated all sectors of church life to the extent that most Black evangelicals, namely Indians and Coloreds, believed it and zealously promoted anti-communism within their congregations. Young pastors, who held views other than the state, were reprimanded with severe consequences. Some were denied ordination. State theology was unfortunately successful in justifying its policies and accusing liberation theology as religious projections of Marxism and Communism. The next chapter will address some of these accusation by exploring liberation theology in order to discover an African meta-narrative of ubuntu liberation.

Conclusion

This chapter addressed the use of the Romans 13 text in South Africa to support Afrikaner ideology and theology. This pericope has been interpreted as an unqualified endorsement of government, giving license for tyrants to justify horrendous abuses of human rights. It has been used by theologians and political leaders to justify various political orders, be they benevolent or oppressive. The chapter carefully explored the biblical text in question and much secondary literature in order to come to an understanding of what the text says. The secondary literature on this text is extensive and is far from exhausted in this study. However, the data presented for this study was sufficient to provide a good

---

83. Moller, *Church Politics*, 21.
84. Ibid., 22.
85. Ibid.
86. Ibid., 20–22.

perspective on this passage and what Paul's intention in writing this section to the Roman Church may have been. The alternative reading reached is closer to the ubuntu idea of humanity because it better respects human equality and dignity, which are too easily neglected in traditional readings.

The chapter was intentional in looking at other possible contexts in which Paul may have written this letter. My conclusions led me to an alternative reading of Romans 13 and a co-opting of Paul to deconstruct South Africa's oppressive meta-narrative. I surveyed the textual authenticity of the passage and examined the passage in the context of the letter and the social make-up of the church in Rome. I explored Paul's teaching as outlined in this passage and discussed how the Afrikaner Church in South Africa utilized this passage to support apartheid. The utilized resources, especially the works of Marcus Borg, Neil Elliott, and Arthur Ogle, provided the helpful insights into the why and what questions proffered at the beginning of this study. In many ways, too, I have supported a "traditional" reading. I have no doubt that Paul wrote this section. I believe that the text was addressed to the church in the capital city of the empire. Although, I think Käsemann's idea that Paul is calling enthusiasts back within the limits of church order and Stuhlmacher's idea that Paul is addressing extortionary practices of tax collectors are viable readings of the particular context for this passage, the certainty of the actual problems will not be known. Thus we must have room to explore other theories based on speculation and circumstantial evidence. Based on my exploration, it seems probable that there was some form of tension or a differing of opinion between the Gentile and Jewish Christians in Rome. It seems as if the Jews had cause to distrust Rome due to what may have been going on in Palestine at the very same time. This may have caused a chasm between Jew and Gentile Christians in Rome. The Roman church was not in harmony, and it is to this particular issue that Paul writes. He is asking the church to submit themselves to church authorities, for God has instituted them, since there is no genuine church authority apart from God.

In the light of this context and intention, governments may apply this text to support their actions notwithstanding that such actions misappropriate God's authority. South Africa and the system of apartheid is an excellent case of how this text can be used to further endeavors that are actually opposed to God's teachings of peace and justice.

3

Discovering an African Meta-Narrative
Ubuntu Liberation

Introduction

IN CHAPTER 1 I LOOKED AT A COMMUNITY OF BELIEVERS STRUGGLING to make sense of the same faith within a context of difference in race, experiences, and resources. In chapter 2 the question was how one group, the Afrikaner, could use Romans 13 to support its oppressive rule of another group, Blacks, within the same community of beliefs. Chapter 3 investigates how the Black South African community of believers, trying to make sense of the Christian faith, discovers a new African meta-narrative of liberation by drawing globally from other oppressed communities. I explore not a top-down model, nor a representation of scripture that is used to support an oppressive model, but rather a model that liberates and supports equality, humanity, dignity, and integrity the ubuntu way. What follows is an exploration of three contexts—Asian, Latin American, and Africa—in which oppressed communities have sought a liberating hermeneutic to make sense of their Christian faith while freeing themselves from an oppressive narrative.

Before the shift of Third World models of interpretation, the Enlightenment model was a monologue: "[T]he Bible speaks to its interpreters who listen. This model of monologue has been displaced by the model of dialogue between text and interpreter because it is evident that what the Bible says is determined . . . by what the interpreter asks."[1] Although First World interpretations are rich with linguistic and historical analysis, they fail to exhaust the meaning of the text completely

---

1. Pope-Levison and Levison, *Jesus in Global Contexts*, 14.

because they ignore contexts that bring their own insights to the process of interpretation. Therefore, in the present chapter I will survey briefly some of the dominant hermeneutical trajectories in so-called two-thirds world contexts and show that Biblical interpretation is incomplete without a global perspective. Although the Bible is comprised of books written to a particular people, for a particular context, and for a particular time, it is only relevant for us today if it is contextualized for our particular contexts.[2]

My exploration of a global perspective in biblical interpretation looks specifically at Latin American liberation theology, Asian Minjung theology, and various African theologies. First, however, I provide a critique of hermeneutics, which will lead to a discussion about why context is necessary for interpretation. The model presented in this chapter is that of multiple conversations. It recognizes that interpreters are drawn to texts that address issues within their interpretive contexts. The present model, leaning heavily on an ubuntu spirituality, also understands conversations to be important for the survival of community and humanity.

Hermeneutics has to do with interpretation of texts. In contemporary discussions however, hermeneutics has become disappointingly unproductive because traditional interpretative models have been exhausted. Terms such as validity, meaning, correctness, application, subjectivity, and objectivity carry assumptions that determine the course of discussion. It is essential to acknowledge that speaking, writing, and interpreting arise within specific contexts. Therefore, the composing and interpreting of texts as actions or sequences of actions must be done under the rubric of responsibility, rather than concerns only with correctness or validity.[3]

Anyone who investigates conflicts in interpretation discovers debates in which the issues are really not interpretive, but rather concern the nature of the interpreter's goals or the effects of a given interpretation on a community that has an interest in the text being interpreted. Hermeneutics is not simply the discussion of a cognitive process whereby we determine the "correct meaning" of a passage or text, but relates to questions of cultural value and social relevance.

---

2. Levison and Pope-Levison, "Global Perspectives," 330–31.
3. Lundin, *Responsibility of Hermeneutics*, x–xi.

"Hermeneutics has traditionally been defined as the study of the locus of meaning and the principles of interpretation."[4] In a broad sense, hermeneutics could be seen as bipolar, exegesis and interpretation. Exegesis is the process of examining a text in an attempt to find out what and how the first readers would have understood it to mean.[5] I. Howard Marshall defines it as, "the attempt to understand anything that somebody else has said or written."[6] In that vein, Chapter 2 concentrated on Romans 13:1–4 in an attempt to understand how the Afrikaner understood the text to support its oppressive policies. Interpretation, on the other hand, is the task of explaining or extracting implications of that understanding for today's readers. I have shown in Chapter 2 how an alternative positive reading of Romans 13 would explain and extract implications that would embrace and not isolate, include and not exclude all of its participants within a community.

One of the essential elements in exegesis is that the interpreter must always approach and analyze a text within its contexts: historical, cultural, geographical, ecclesiastical, ideological, or literary. On can consider three stages in the interpretative process: the event, the recording of the event in a text, and the reading of the text. Each stage is separated by time. For Scripture, this gap between the recording of the event and the reading of the text is centuries. While the text has not changed, the language and culture of readers do. The interpreter will impose his or her understanding of the contemporary world upon the text. The task of contextual study is to narrow the gap between the original readers and the modern ones. Since the biblical authors wrote out of a particular context and culture, proclaiming a particular culturally conditioned message to a culturally identified audience, the modern reader must attempt to return to that context.[7] Mickelsen affirms this claim when he states,

> The interpreter . . . stands in a modern culture, whether this be Western or another. He must understand the particular biblical culture, which influenced the original source, message, and receptors. He must note both how it differs from and how it

---

4. Tate, *Biblical Interpretation*, xv.
5. Ibid., xix.
6. Marshall, "Introduction," 11.
7. Tate, *Biblical Interpretation*, 29–30.

resembles his own. Only then can he effectively communicate the message from one culture pattern to another.[8]

The task for Christians today is to embody Scripture in the various contexts in which they find themselves. Discerning how to go about embodying Scripture however is a complex exercise. The result of this complexity is clearly one of contexts. The context in which the Bible was originally written and the variety of contemporary contexts in which Christians live and read Scripture is different. Professional biblical scholarship has made this point with considerable power. It is this issue of contexts that fundamentalistic attempts to follow simply the demands of Scripture in the present fails to articulate adequately the relationship between Scripture and the contemporary Christian life.[9] Lash illustrates this point clearly:

> If, in thirteenth-century Italy, you wandered around in a coarse brown gown, with a cord around your middle, your social location was clear: your dress said that you were one of the poor. If, in twentieth-century Cambridge, you wander around in a coarse brown gown, with a cord around your middle, your social location is curious: your dress now says, not that you are one of the poor, but that you are some kind of oddity in the business of religion. Your dress now declares not your solidarity with the poor, but your amiable eccentricity.[10]

Lash points to the necessity for ongoing dialogue about how to continue a tradition in spite of temporal and cultural change. One may also infer that while there certainly is temporal distance between the settings of Scripture and one's own, more important complexities are not necessarily historical, but rather moral and theological. An important task for Christians today is to develop a moral and theological judgment that enables faithful discernment of Scripture's claims on contemporary life.

Stephen Fowl and Gregory Jones contend that there is no way of understanding texts apart from particular social contexts. We do not come to the text or make decisions as isolated individuals or in a vacuum. We come as people with particular histories, commitments,

---

8. Mickelsen, *Interpreting the Bible*, 170.
9. Fowl and Jones, *Reading in Communion*, 1.
10. Lash, "What," 54.

habits, dispositions, and convictions. The way we evaluate issues, texts, and our lives is shaped by the kinds of people we are and want to become. Obedience to rules and the way we assess consequences surely play a role; but Fowl and Jones remind us that the community of readers consists of the "context of people exercising the virtues of character, as those have been shaped and nurtured by particular communities that are the social embodiment of a tradition's moral vision."[11]

Conversations can be unsettling. The first White South African to live in a Black township recalls an unsettling conversation he had with the great Swiss theologian Karl Barth in the mid-1960s. At the time of the conversation, Nico Smith was a proponent of apartheid and a member of the Broederbund, an exclusive secret Afrikaner nationalist organization. Barth asked Smith, "Tell me, are you free to preach the gospel in South Africa?" "Of course!" Smith replied. "We have freedom of religion in South Africa." "No," Barth retorted, "that is not the type of freedom I am asking about. Are you free in yourself? Say, for instance, you became convinced of a certain meaning of the gospel which might not be the way your family and friends understand the gospel. Would you feel free to say, 'this is how I understand the gospel and how I must preach it'?" Continuing to press the point, Barth added: "You may arrive at a point where your convictions about the gospel contradict what your government believes. Will you then also feel free to preach the gospel?" Barth's questions plagued Nico Smith as he began to wonder whether he was free to preach against apartheid. Eventually, in 1982, the conversation with Barth contributed to his becoming the pastor of the Black Dutch Reformed Church located in the Black township of Mamelodi.[12]

The nineteenth-century Enlightenment model has dominated biblical scholarship for almost two centuries. In it, a scholar's task is to understand the original meaning of the text by utilizing linguistic and historical analysis. This approach calls for the interpreter to suspend all biases in order not to uncover the original meaning with modern questions. Is this possible? Can an interpreter understand the text without biases or prejudgments formed from his or her own context? The

---

11. Fowl and Jones, *Reading in Communion*, 13.

12. Pope-Levison and Levison, *Jesus in Global Contexts*, 11. I have heard Nico Smith recount this story several times particularly to drive the point that conversations are unsettling. In Green, ed., *Hearing the New Testament*, the authors collectively make a similar point: the model for interpretation is that of a conversation.

Enlightenment model has been called into question and must be treated with suspicion.[13]

The Necessity for Context in Interpretation

Another model of interpretation is available, a model based on the belief that deepest insight and relevance is not found in the "original meaning" of the Bible, nor in the contemporary context, but in the to-and-fro of question and answer between them. There is an historical tradition or context that we all belong to and this limits our viewpoint or perspective; therefore, in the active engagement between interpreter and text one's own horizon is shaped or re-shaped because the interpreter cannot fully distance oneself from that historical tradition in which he or she belongs. Thus, this fusion of horizons will not become identical but at best will remain separate but close. In an engagement with the Bible, interpreters become partners in conversation with the text, addressing questions that may arise from the context in which they may find themselves. This conversation with interpreter and text will develop a life of its own.[14] Indeed, such an idea resonates with the idea of ubuntu, the absolute necessary interconnected relatedness between one with the other—the text being one and the context the other. The fusing of the horizons is a conversation between the past and present that develops a relevant interpretation.

Theologians such as Bultmann, Lonergan, and Tracy confirm that the context of interpreters inevitably shapes their approaches to literary texts. The fact is that no interpreter enters into the attempt to understand any text or historical event without prejudgments formed by the history of the effects of his or her culture. There does not exist any exegete or historian as purely autonomous as the Enlightenment model promised.[15]

Support for contextual Christology can be found in the implication that, "the modern interpreter, no less than the text, stands in a given historical context and tradition."[16] Context must be the starting point for theological reflection. The contexts for theology must include political,

13. Levison and Pope-Levison, "Global Perspectives," 329.
14. See Thiselton, *Two Horizons*, xix.
15. Grant and Tracy, *A Short History*, 156.
16. Thiselton, *The Two Horizons*, 11.

economic, social, religious, and cultural factors. No theological method is adequate apart from a critical analysis, which looks seriously into the factors mentioned above, since these factors provide the only accurate understanding of our particular contexts.[17] Since every interpretation is a fusion of the text and context, no one interpretation is universal because of the uniqueness of each context. McAfee Brown encapsulates two important theses of context for theology: 1) all theologies are contextually conditioned, and 2) it may take others to show us how conditioned, parochial, or ideologically captive our own theology is.[18]

According to McAfee Brown's first thesis, any attempt to universalize theology is denounced, and any claim to do theology on behalf of another context is eradicated, since all theologies and theologians are influenced by and committed to a specific context and social location. In line with his second thesis, two-thirds world theologies are attempting to demonstrate to the first world that western theology is captive to its own context. Western theology is founded in western traditions and philosophy with a western systematic approach. Though geographically localized and culturally conditioned, western interpretations became "universalized" because western theology itself had become "the" theology of the Church. Two-thirds world theologians charge that western theology is not in fact a universal theology, but rather a predominantly European theology. Edward Schillebeeckx admits, "with the emergence of liberation theology... Western theologians came to the realization that their own theology has just as much socio-cultural bias as any other."[19] The development of Black, Hispanic, and Amerindian theologies in the United States, theologies arising in the complex contexts of Africa, Asia, and the South Pacific, and the especially fruitful thinking of those who have adopted the feminist perspective has meant that for the first time in many centuries theology is being done outside the customary European and North American centers. The result in the so-called First World has been a new kind of dialogue between traditional thinking and newer, contextualized models of understanding.[20] The change in the center of gravity, according to Walls, "is no longer in Europe, decreasingly in

---

17. Pope-Levison and Levison, *Jesus in Global Contexts*, 15.
18. Brown, "Diversity," 52–53.
19. Schillebeeckx, "Foreword," ix.
20. Gutiérrez, *A Theology of Liberation*, xix.

North America, but in Latin America, in certain parts of Asia, and most important for our present purposes, in Africa."[21]

In Chapter 2 we saw how liberation theology was viewed as evil cloaked in religious garb. The liberationist's move away from the traditional or literal reading of the text was viewed by the Afrikaner as influenced by Marxist ideology, which opened the doors to the infiltration of communism. Thus, in light of the preceding discussion about the necessity for contexts in interpretation, it seems relevant to discuss more thoroughly the hermeneutics of liberation.

Hermeneutics of Liberation

Latin American Liberation Theology

To understand the hermeneutics of liberation, one needs to be aware of and appreciate the cycles of life, death, and struggle in the communities from which it emerges. The Peruvian priest, Gustavo Gutiérrez, provides the most authoritative starting point for its fundamental principles. At the Medellin Conference in 1968, Gutiérrez and other Latin American theologians motivated the Conference to "make the needs of the Latin American poor a critical element in their theological thinking. This entailed emphasizing the theological importance of engagement with the Latin American social context."[22]

Gutiérrez's foundational work, *A Theology of Liberation*, founded a new direction and form for theological reflection, which clearly expressed the central theme of the theological challenge in Latin America. He writes, "To speak about a theology of liberation is to seek an answer to the following question: what relation is there between salvation and the historical process of human liberation?"[23]

HERMENEUTICAL PRINCIPLES

Two key principles that shape liberation theology can be discerned from Gutiérrez's work: 1) a theological method in which theology proper is always a "second act" after a commitment to liberation, and 2) the need to make an "option for the poor" and articulate theology from this per-

21. Walls, "Towards Understanding," 180.
22. Tombs, "The Hermeneutics of Liberation," 313–14.
23. Gutiérrez, *A Theology of Liberation*, 29.

spective. Therefore, most liberation emphasize the historical concerns as an essential starting point as a second act in liberation theology. The church must understand theology as critical reflection on prior commitment and that theology is a reflection, a second act that comes after action. Theology is not first; commitment is first. Hence, theology is merely the understanding of that commitment and that commitment is action.

Gutiérrez also demonstrates how liberation is the integral relationship between salvation and history. He perceives salvation and temporal realms of history and politics as inseparable. Joseph Cardinal Ratzinger (now Pope Benedict XVI), who was for over two decades the Prefect for the Congregation for the Doctrine of the Faith under Pope John Paul II, was one of the most prominent critics of liberation theology, later denouncing theologians such as Leonardo Boff.[24] These theologians are quick to allege that liberation theologians attempt to equate salvation with political liberation. However, support for this claim is difficult to find in Gutiérrez's work, since he "distinguishes between the three levels of liberation and stresses that together they form a single complex process: first, at the economic and political level, liberation applies to oppressed peoples and social classes; secondly, at the existential level of human freedom, liberation applies to people taking conscious responsibility for their own historical destiny; finally, at the theological level, liberation is understood as liberation from sin."[25]

Theology springs from spirituality in an attempt to meet God in history. Liberation theology is the result of faith confronting injustice done to the poor. "By poor we do not really mean the poor individual who knocks on the door asking for alms. We mean a collective poor, the popular classes, which is a much wider category than the proletariat singled out by Karl Marx."[26] Boff cautions "that it would be a mistake to identify the poor of liberation theology with the proletariat, though many of its critics do."[27] For liberation theologians, the poor includes "workers exploited by the capitalist system; the underemployed, those pushed aside by the production process with a reserve army always at

---

24. See Ratzinger, *The Ratzinger Report*.
25. Tombs, "The Hermeneutics of Liberation," 314–17.
26. Boff and Boff, *Introducing Liberation Theology*, 3.
27. Ibid.

hand to take the place of the employed; they are the laborers of the countryside and migrant workers with only seasonal work."[28]

Opting for the poor is not an option; it is a clear command of the Gospels. The Gospels depicts Jesus's life as one of self-chosen poverty (Matt 8:20; Luke 9:58). The disciples left all in order to follow him (Matt 4:18; Mark 1:16–20; Luke 5:1–11, John 1:35–51). The sale of his possessions and a life of discipleship in poverty were demanded of the rich young ruler as a precondition of eternal life (Matt 19:16–22; Luke 18:18–24). The lifestyle that Jesus adopted for himself and called his disciples to adopt was one that exemplified the Sermon on the Mount, especially the Beatitudes. His whole way of life was a conscious identification with the poor. Rather than a prophetic announcement of siding with the oppressed, the challenge for Christians today is what strategies and development would they pursue that would make a difference if they are to serve the poor effectively and lift the poor out of poverty.[29] Liberation theology can only be understood in the light of suffering. Underlying liberation theology is the commitment to, comradeship with, and proclamation to the "life, cause, and struggle of...debased and marginalized human beings, a commitment to ending this historical social iniquity."[30] Reflection on the social issues that affect the two-thirds world is not just an academic exercise with detached observation and abstract reflection common to European and North American models in theological thought. Instead it requires commitment to the liberation of the oppressed.[31] The Vatican Instruction of August 6, 1984, sums up the aspects of liberation theology well:

> It is not possible for a single instant to forget the situations of dramatic poverty from which the challenge set to theologians springs the challenge to work out a genuine theology of liberation.[32]

Critics such as Cardinal Alfonso Lopez Trujillo, Roger Vekemanns, The International Theological Commission appointed by the Vatican made up predominately of European theologians in 1974, Cardinal

28. Ibid., 3–4.
29. Sherman, *Preferential Option*, 219.
30. Boff and Boff, *Introducing Liberation Theology*, 3.
31. Tombs, "The Hermeneutics of Liberation," 316.
32. Cited in Boff and Boff, *Introducing Liberation Theology*, 3.

Joseph Ratzinger, Thomas G. Sanders, and Dennis McCann have posed some of the strongest opposition to liberation theology and Gutierrez's belief that humanity can save itself from its sinful situation. They say that salvation in terms of development and reform is risky because it does not emphasize the theological conviction that salvation is dependent on God's grace as well as human response. They further criticize his oversimplifying the theological nature of salvation by representing it purely in terms of human liberation struggles and equating theology with politics.[33] Two elements of his seminal work are used to support these claims. First, Gutiérrez primarily deals with liberation from political and economic oppression. Later, his understanding of liberation is understood as liberation from sin. The result is a view of sinfulness limited to the political/economic level. Second, Gutiérrez describes his theology as a "political hermeneutic of the Gospel."[34] However, even though one can easily interpret his theology as a political hermeneutic, upon a closer reading and understanding of his theology, his emphasis on politics is more a critique of the establishment and institutions set in place that should be working for the people and not a hindrance to their freedom and liberation. Hence, his emphasis is more a corrective, an appeal to the powers that be, rather than a neglect of all the other aspects of theology that affect the Christian life. He emphasizes his meaning of salvation in which all three levels of liberation introduced earlier—namely the economic and political level; the existential level of human freedom; and the theological level—are essential and inseparable from each other. Therefore, when he talks about the political level, he does so not with disregard for all the other dimensions that effect human beings but instead he takes them more seriously in that unless the political structures change to heed to the needs of the poor, the disenfranchised, the oppressed, the existential and the theological levels are incomplete and ineffective to the fullness of salvation.[35]

Liberation theology has also been criticized for its commitment to violence. Critics point to the active participation of Christians in Central America (for example, Nicaragua's attempt to overthrow Somoza in 1979 and Camilo Torres's participation with guerilla groups) as cases

---

33. For a more detailed critique of Liberation Theology see McGovern, *Liberation Theology*.

34. Tombs, "The Hermeneutics of Liberation," 320.

35. Ibid., 320–21.

for liberation theology's commitment to violence.³⁶ These however, are exceptions and not the rule. To equate liberation theology to guerilla groups reduces its theologies to extremes and is similar to representing Islam with the examples of Osama Bin Laden and Al Quaeda only. Similarly, in the South African context, there were always militant groups who used violence in their approach to overthrow the racist Afrikaner apartheid regime. These were Christians who attended political meetings where Bishop Tutu would call for non-violent strategies as the only option for a Christian engagement in the anti-apartheid dialogue, yet they engaged in violent activities outside of those meetings. This did not mean that Tutu's theology included calls to violence; though the apartheid government and Dutch Reformed Christians have tried to make that association.

The preferential option for the poor in liberation theology has its roots in the failure of churches, academic theologians, and biblical scholars in Europe and North America to address the issues of injustice worldwide. Since much theology and biblical scholarship is done in the comfortable settings of research institutions, university libraries, and pleasant offices, with the security of grants and research fellowships— present work included!—it is hard to identify with the real-world needs of the majority of humanity. An effective commitment to liberation must be guided by a shift in social perspective. Theologians must re-read the world and the word from the position of the poor.³⁷

"Aid" offered by individuals and nations is often nothing more than a "band-aid" or "corn-plaster" approach and remains a strategy to treat the poor as objects of charity, not subjects of their own liberation. It fails to see that the poor are oppressed and made poor by others,

---

36. The references are to Nicaragua's attempt to overthrow its forty-fourth and forty-fifth President Anastasio Somoza Debayle, who ruled from May 1, 1967 to May 1, 1972 and from December 1, 1974 to July 17, 1979. He was the last member of the Somoza family to be President, ending a dynasty that had held power since 1936. The younger son of dictator Anastasio Somoza García, Debayle assumed command of the national guard at age 21 and was elected president in 1967. Barred from immediate re-election, he resigned in 1972, nominally yielding power until the 1974 elections; however, as commander of the corrupt and brutal national guard, he effectively retained power. As president, he dealt ruthlessly with opposition and by the late 1970's, his regime was denounced by human-rights organizations and by the U.S. government, and support for violent insurrection spread. See further Tombs, *Latin American Liberation Theology*, 52.

37. Tombs, "The Hermeneutics of Liberation," 322.

and that they do possess things such as strength to resist, capacity to understand rights, ability to organize themselves and transform a subhuman situation. Aid, according to Boff and Boff, increases the dependency of the poor to others, thus not enabling them to become their own liberators.[38]

Reformism on the other hand, attempts to improve the situation of the poor within existing social relationships of the structures of society. Such an approach rules out participation by all and the diminution of the privileges enjoyed by the ruling classes. Even reformism's developmental strategies for the poor are almost always at the expense of the poor. The price paid by the poor for this type of elitist, exploitative, and exclusivist development just causes the rich to become richer at the expense of the poor who become poorer.[39]

In summary, the commitment to liberation and the preferential option for the poor, according to Tombs, provides the fundamental principles for a new starting point and criteria for theology.[40] Engagement with the social issues and solidarity with the poor forms the framework for understanding liberation theology. Theologians and biblical scholars must recognize these fundamental principles as paramount. These issues are not raised just in order to reform the shortcomings of traditional models of theology. It is not enough to give more attention to the themes of liberation and oppression in Bible studies; liberation theologians call for a whole new direction in doing theology. The biblical themes of poverty, oppression, and liberation require a new theological method, for a proper understanding of the gospel is inseparable from an active response to it.

Methodology and Marxism

Having located the fundamental hermeneutical principles of liberation theology, I turn to reflections on two documents, which were the most influential for the development of liberation theology: The Vatican II document, *Gaudium et Spes* (Pastoral Constitution on the Church in the Modern World), and the documents of the Medellín Conference

---

38. Boff and Boff, *Introducing Liberation Theology*, 4–5.
39. Ibid.
40. Tombs, "The Hermeneutics of Liberation," 323–24.

(1968).⁴¹ The reflections will lead us to a discussion of liberation methodology and its association with Marxist ideas. For the Roman Catholic Church, *Gaudium et Spes* opened the window for criticism of Marxism and its social analysis the widest. The three-step methodology of this document has been as influential as many of its conclusions.

An elaboration of liberation theology can be divided into these three basic steps: seeing, judging, and acting.⁴² Cleary describes this three-step process as facts, reflection, and recommendations,⁴³ while Boff and Boff speak of this method as mediations: socio-analytical mediation, hermeneutical meditation, and practical meditation.⁴⁴ The Boffs use "mediation" because the three stages represent "means" or "instruments" of the theological process. These mediations work as follows:

- Socio-analytical (or historico-analytical) mediation operates in the sphere of the world of the oppressed. It tries to find out why the oppressed are oppressed.
- Hermeneutical mediation operates in the sphere of God's world. It tries to discern what God's plan is for the poor.
- Practical mediation operates in the sphere of action. It tries to discover the courses of action that need to be followed so as to overcome oppression in accordance with God's plan.⁴⁵

The first step begins with a social and economic analysis of the Latin American situation. The context is analyzed using the tools of social and behavioral sciences, as well as economic theory. Step two continues with biblical and theological reflection on the contextual reality. Step three concludes with recommendations for how the Latin American church can be in solidarity with the poor.

In the first two mediations, Marxist ideas are used as instruments for social analysis. Marx used the term "praxis," which he defined as a

---

41. For the full English text of *Gaudium et Spes* see http://www.vatican.va/archive/hist_councils/ii_vatican_council/documents/vat-ii_cons_19651207_gaudium-et-spes_en.html. For English excerpts of the Medellín documents see http://www.providence.edu/las/documents.htm#Medell%EDn%20Conference.
42. Pope-Levison and Levison, *Jesus in Global Contexts*, 28.
43. Cleary, *Crisis and Change*, 22.
44. Boff and Boff, *Introducing Liberation Theology*.
45. Boff and Boff, *Introducing Liberation Theology*, 24.

concrete engagement for the purpose of transformation.[46] Liberation theologians use the term to mean, "transforming action."[47] By this, they point to a historical transformation, a transforming change, or transforming action of history. Praxis for liberation theologians is action on behalf of the poor. They assume a pre-commitment for the poor. This pre-commitment reverses theology as it has traditionally been done. Rather than the normal utilization of theological foundations, terminology, Bible, and church traditions, liberation theology begins with praxis among the poor. Theology reflects on this praxis, which then leads to a renewed praxis for further theological reflections.[48]

In utilizing Marxist social analysis to investigate their contexts, two conclusions are derived. First, a class struggle exists between the majority working class and the minority owning class. Second, liberation is the solution to the class struggle. "Liberation theologians demand 'integral liberation,' that touches all forms of oppression, that is, political and economic injustice, social indignity among the marginalized of society, and sin, which divides God from humankind and neighbor from neighbor."[49]

Critics such as the Vatican, Cardinal Ratzinger, Enrique Colom Casta, Roger Vekemans, and Jose Luis Illanes—to name a few—have interpreted the Christian options for the poor and oppressed and the use of Marxist analysis as a Marxist manipulation or infiltration of theology. When liberation theology was initially formulated "development" was the catchword of the times for the amelioration of the Latin American situation.[50] President Kennedy's aid program known as the "Alliance for Progress" was an attempt to develop Latin America economically, socially, and politically. This however raised dissonant voices among liberation theologians expressing that development will soon lead to dependency on foreign aid and will ultimately lead to the cause of its poverty and underdevelopment. They believed that dependence

---

46. This understanding of praxis comes from Marx's eleventh thesis on Feuerbach: "The philosophers have only interpreted the world, in various ways; the point is to change it." Marx and Engels, *Basic Writings*, 245. See also Pope-Levinson and Levinson, *Jesus in Global Contexts*, 50n12.

47. See Gutiérrez, "Statement."

48. Pope-Levison and Levison, *Jesus in Global Contexts*, 30–31.

49. Levison and Pope-Levison, "Global Perspectives," 331–32.

50. Pope-Levison and Levison, *Jesus in Global Contexts*, 33.

on foreign powers would be used to keep Latin America in a condition of underdevelopment and this dependency will lead to subordination and loss of autonomy.[51] Instead, "development" was replaced with "liberation" to signify a break from dependent relationships and ineffective development programs. In light of the Cuban Revolution of 1959, and the killings of Camilo Torres and Ernesto "Che" Guevara, who attempted liberation through guerrilla movements, "liberation" as used by the Latin American theologians of the Medellín Conference implied a revolutionary break from national-developmental reformism as well as new military regimes. It is within this specific historical context that we must understand the shift from a theology of development to a theology of liberation.[52]

The theology of development was pre-Marxist, while the theology of revolution used Marxist instruments of analysis in ways different from liberation theology. Historically, the difference between the theology of development and the theology of revolution was in the "presence or absence of a theory of dependency, which Latin-Americanized Marxism and gave it a historico-social dimension. Let us not forget where it all started: with Jose Profirio Miranda's historic Marx and the Bible, which posed the question forthrightly and biblically. But paradoxically, what we have, is a Christian looking at Marx, and not actually a Marxist interpretation of the encounter between Marx and theology."[53]

According to Arthur McGovern, Hugo Assmann, considered to be the most Marxist of liberation theologians, said, "liberation theology confronts problems arising from dependence, exploitation, and imperialism," and that the capitalist system is the root cause of problem.[54] Thus, as Assmann concludes, "Talking of liberation implies taking a new analytical stance with regard to the situation of our countries, a basically new conception of the phenomenon of under-development, and consequently, a new point of departure from which to map out the political and economic ways out of this situation. The conclusions drawn are inevitably revolutionary, and the language of liberation is the

---

51. McGovern, *Liberation Theology*, 165.
52. Ibid., 33–34.
53. Dussel, "Theology of Liberation," 89.
54. McGovern, *Liberation Theology*, 140.

language that articulates them. This relates it directly to the new analysis of under-development."[55]

At a 1978 national meeting addressing delegates from base communities in Brazil, Leonardo Boff affirms that, "the main root of this oppression is the elitist, exclusive, capitalist system." In August 1987 for the National Catholic Reporter, both Leonardo and Clodovis Boff criticized the U.S. Catholic Bishops pastoral letter on the U.S. Economy for not calling into question the system of capitalism. They said, "Capitalism can be more or less immoral; it can never be more or less moral. It is just impossible to create a moral market system as it is to build a Christian brothel."[56] The Boffs' rejection of capitalism is oriented to liberation in the framework of a different society. Theology is constructed from two starting points: faith and social reality. To rediscover this reality, while remaining faithful to theological reflection, "recourse must be had to the human social sciences, such as anthropology, sociology, psychology, political science, economics, and social philosophy."[57]

Marxism is adopted by the theology of liberation as a model that not only interprets reality, but also justifies its transformation. The Vatican in its attempt to bring liberation theologians into line with ecclesial authority, Cardinal Ratzinger as Prefect for Doctrine and Faith put out the Instruction on Certain Aspects of the Theology of Liberation in 1984. In this document, liberation theology stood accused on two grounds. First, it is wrongfully committed to the idea of class conflict and the necessity of violence presented in Marxist social analysis. Second, in accepting ideas of Marxist social analysis, liberation theology commits itself to an atheistic philosophy and a "reductionist reading of the Bible."[58] Liberation theologians, however, argue that upon reading Marx apart from Engels, Lenin, and Stalin, there are no traces of accusations such as "Atheism and the rejection of the human person, of his freedom and his rights, are at the center of the Marxist conception. On the contrary, Marx actually opposed the militant atheism of the Communist international." Liberation theologians have been able to remove from Marxism

---

55. Assmann, *Theology for a Nomad Church*, 130.
56. McGovern, *Liberation Theology*, 138–39.
57. Gorgulho, "Biblical Hermeneutics," 130.
58. Tombs, "The Hermeneutics of Liberation," 347.

elements that are incompatible with their faith.⁵⁹ Gutiérrez and others do not use Marxism as an uncritical allegiance to its philosophy. It is used only to draw from its analysis ideas that serve the cause of the poor by illuminating the real causes of their oppression.⁶⁰

Asian Minjung Theology

From the islands of the Philippines to the Himalayas, Asia encompasses both the affluence of Tokyo to the poverty of Calcutta, while at the same time holding in tension the vast and diverse varieties of Islam, Christianity, Hinduism, and Buddhism. In spite of this diversity, three hermeneutical trends in theology can be found in this region. As with liberation theologians of Latin America, the social reality of the Asian people is the starting point for many Asian theologians. They reflect people's folktales, stories, and artistic expressions theologically.

Korean minjung theologians consider the social biographies of the "mass of the people" or *minjung*. Indeed, Choan-Seng Song calls the minjung perspective, a "people hermeneutic" where the Bible functions as a mirror of social biography when it is juxtaposed with expressions that are common to the Asian reality.⁶¹ Social biographers of the minjung can include people who are from among the poor, farmers, workers, intellectuals, and students. A social biography can include artistic expressions such as dance and drama that portray the people's oppression and ridicule the people's oppressors.⁶² Minjung theology is one of the most provocative and challenging theologies to emerge in recent years. Like the artistic expressions of social biography, minjung theologians take as their starting-point for doing theology and reading the Bible, the contextual realities of the minjung, the people who are politically oppressed, socially alienated, economically exploited, and kept uneducated in cultural and intellectual matters.⁶³

In a recent essay Byung-Mu Ahn attempts to re-read "the crowd," ὁ ὄχλος, in Mark's Gospel from the perspective of Korean minjung

---

59. Dussel, "Theology of Liberation," 93–94.
60. Tombs, "The Hermeneutics of Liberation," 348.
61. Song, *Jesus, the Crucified People*, 12.
62. Levison and Pope-Levison, "Global Perspectives," 334.
63. Ahn, "Jesus and the Minjung," 85.

theology.⁶⁴ He demonstrates how historical-critical tools can be used to liberate biblical texts. He argues that New Testament scholarship has focused much attention on the people who are the audience and the object of Jesus' teaching; however, little attention has been paid to the social character of his audience. Thus, the words and deeds of Jesus have been de-socialized. To get at the social characteristic of Jesus' teaching, one needs to investigate the economic, political, and cultural make-up of the people. In other words, a more comprehensive understanding of the social structure and place of people's surrounding must be the focus.

Form critics, according to Ahn, focus on the editorial sections about the people that surround Jesus as only a framework for the words of Jesus or for the kerygma that Jesus is the Christ. Therefore, he argues, the people have been excluded which resulted in the loss of a very important aspect. Likewise, redaction critics consider the redactional framework important for understanding the viewpoint of the author and the import of Jesus' sayings in context, but little attention have been given to the audience of the people. Ahn seems to suggest that both form and redactional critics seem to miss the point in that they pay more attention to the theology of the authors of the Gospels. But rather, the authors of the Gospels actually put more emphasis on the people. It is the relationship between the people and Jesus is what is most crucial for a thorough understanding of the identity and mission of Jesus.⁶⁵

Ahn argues that Mark deliberately avoids the term λαός and uses the term ὄχλος to indicate the minjung, the mass of people. He differentiates between the people of God, who are those within the national and religious framework as defined by the Pharisees, and the minjung. The minjung do not belong to the national and religious framework as defined by the Pharisees, nor are they the repented, who have become the new people of God. The minjung belong to a class of society who have been abandoned and marginalized. They are minjung not because they have a common destiny, but because they are alienated, dispossessed, and powerless. They are not represented as a class that has a

---

64. Ibid., 85–104.

65. Ibid., 85–86. Ahn argues that Mark was the first writer to introduce the term o1xloj. It does not appear in the New Testament before Mark. Whereas Paul focuses on a highly kerygmatic theology, Mark moves toward a historical theology, thus developing a theology of the people.

power base. They are different from the people in the Gospel of John who sought to crown Jesus as a king.[66]

"People are clues to who the real Jesus is—people who are poor, outcast, and socially and politically oppressed. What Jesus has said and done is not comprehensible apart from men, women, and children who suffer in body and spirit."[67] The life and work of Jesus grows out of the close relationship developed between him and the people, the minjung. Therefore, for Song, Christological hermeneutics has to be a people's hermeneutic.[68] The messianic contours of Jesus becomes increasingly sharpened as he absorbs himself into the struggle of the people.

According to minjung theology, "God is seen in the story of Jesus, and Jesus is found in the story of the people. He is the pain of God mingled with the pain of humanity. He is the hope of God that people manifest in the midst of despair. He is the eternal life of God in which people live despite death. Jesus is, lives, and becomes real when people, with unflagging faith in God, engage each other to bring about a New World out of the ruins of the Old World ... And being the story of such people, Jesus is the story of God."[69]

Ahn relates a story that illustrates well the crux of minjung theology:

> Chi-Ha Kim, a Korean poet, wrote a play titled the Gold-Crowned Jesus. The scene plays in front of a Catholic Church, where a statue of Jesus, made of cement, is to be found. On his head he is wearing a golden crown. Below the statue there are beggars lying around. The time is early morning on a cold winter's day.
>
> As time passes, first a pot-bellied priest and then a fat man, looking like the boss of a company, walk by ... the beggars ask for alms again and again, but are refused with contempt and scorn.... Eventually a policeman...drives them out of the place and demands a fine from them in return for his connivance. After all of them are gone, one of the beggars starts to lament: "I have neither home, nor grave to rest from all the exhaustion ... I cannot endure it any longer ...." As he so laments himself in despair, his eyes, filled with tears, meet the cement statue of Jesus

---

66. Ibid., 101–2.
67. Song, *Jesus, the Crucified People*, 12.
68. Ibid.
69. Song, *Jesus*, 12–14.

> ... With a critical glance at the statue—grumbles in his mind: "This Jesus might well be a savior to those who have enough to eat, who have a home and a family. But what good has he done for a beggar like me?" ... How on earth can Jesus speak without a mouth? Can a lump of cement speak ...
>
> Crying out loudly, the beggar...begins to weep. Right at that moment he feels something wet, like small drops falling on his head. Is it raining? No!—When he looks up he finds the cement Jesus weeping and dropping tears. He watches Jesus intently, and only then does he realize that Jesus is wearing a golden crown ... Having found that that is real gold, the idea crosses his mind that if he sold the crown, he would have enough to eat and something to live on ... he grasps the crown and takes it off. At this very moment he hears a voice: "Take it, please! For too long time have I been imprisoned in this cement. ... I wish to talk with poor people like you and share your suffering ... I have been waiting for this day to come—the day of my liberation when I could once again flare up like a candle and bring light to your misery ... It's you who saved me. These are the words spoken by the gold-crowned Jesus.[70]

The very thing that makes Jesus turn into cement is the Christology of the Church. The minjung cry, talk of the crown of Jesus, hear his voice, and see his tears. Within the structures of traditional Christology, they experience a Jesus confined to the cement. By becoming aware of the existence and realities of the minjung in the Gospels minjung theologians hope to set free the Jesus imprisoned in the cement statue. They cannot do this by the intellectual analysis of the Bible alone; they will need the help of the minjung.[71]

For minjung theologians, the historical Jesus is preferred to the Christ of the kerygma. Stress on the Christ of the kerygma by many western New Testament scholars is perceived as a roadblock to the historical Jesus. Minjung theology hits on an important hermeneutical point with regards to finding the historical Jesus; it makes the people the savior of the historical Jesus. The beggar saves Jesus. Some people may find hard to accept and problematic that the historical Jesus is given more prominence to the Christian faith than the resurrected Christ, which is used as a major difference between Christianity and other

---

70. Ahn, "Jesus and People," 163–64.
71. Ibid., 165.

religions. Minjung theology, however, returns to the importance of the historical Jesus and in finding the real essence of what he was about. In this way, Jesus, the liberator, becomes once again alive and no longer just a historical figure.

The cross for the Christian faith is the supreme symbol of God's suffering love. In the cross, suffering is not merely physical, institutional, impersonal, or secular. It is religious, human, and divine. The lotus is to Buddhists what the cross is to Christians. Though different in many ways, these two symbols point to a crucial quest of human life and deliverance. "Without the cross the faith inculcated by the humble carpenter from Nazareth would have dissipated soon after his death. By the same token, without the lotus and what it tries to communicate, the lofty teachings of Buddhism would have probably failed to captivate the devotion of the masses."[72] Likewise, without the lotus, Buddhism would have failed to captivate the devotion of the masses. Out of these two symbols, two distinct cultures and religions were born, the culture of the cross, and the culture of the lotus.[73]

From the perspective of Christian missionaries, the spirituality of the lotus was atheistic in teaching and idolatrous in practice. The encounter of these two religions and cultures took a sinister turn in the battlefields of Vietnam in 1963. For the Vietnamese, what was an opposition to President Ngo Dinh Diem was an opposition to Christianity.

> For us Vietnamese, to embrace Christianity means that we would be forbidden to worship our Ancestors, our deceased parents, when this has been the most important thing in our style of life for thousands of years . . . The Christians are hybrids . . . they are absurd with regard to Vietnamese thought. Nor is their language even Vietnamese . . . The young Vietnamese want to know why there are so many differences between Christianity and their culture, why this religion is so contrary to their Volkgeist . . . why this severity and cruelty of the Almighty God who unceasingly curses and threatens men and women with such horrible words while that God ought to be saving them.[74]

72. Song, *Third-Eye Theology*, 101.

73. Ibid., 119–20. This equality of religion, symbolism, and freedom will be explored further in Chapter 5 with South Africa's meta-narrative of ubuntu freeing apartheid's Christian hegemony to religious pluralism.

74. Gheddo, *The Cross and the Bo-tree*, 242–43.

These questions were directed to the Catholic Church, since President Diem was counted as one of the members of this church. This sentiment that the spirituality of the lotus as being atheistic in teaching and idolatrous in practice is a clear indication of distortion, misrepresentation, and abuse of the spirituality of the lotus versus the spirituality of the cross by Christian missionaries. Christian missionary endeavors have missed the symbolism of idols and images in other religions. A statue of Buddha in London, to most western viewers, is no more than an object of aesthetic curiosity, just as a crucifix to people in a remote village in Asia who have never come into contact with Christianity cannot be a symbol representing God's love for the world.[75]

Since the "people hermeneutic" of minjung emerges from the Asian people, there is no strict model that determines any one meaning of the Bible. A resonance rather than a restricted meaning of the Bible juxtaposes the Asian social biography and the New Testament. Therefore, biblical interpreters seek to draw parallels between the Bible and other sacred writings by employing comparative textual studies. Economics, too, is an aspect of the Asian reality that plays into the biblical exploration. Some Asian theologians even utilize Marxist social analysis, though not as wholeheartedly as Latin American theologians.[76]

Asian Buddhists enter human suffering through the lotus, and Christians through the cross. They have a common entry into the ultimate question of life, which is suffering, and they share a common duty to go together through suffering with faith and hope in the salvation of all humanity.[77]

African Theologies

The Bible, though written by one people, the Jews, has become a universal book. Its connection to the continent of Africa is seen not only in the fact that some key events of the Bible took place in Africa, but also in the fact that the first translation of the Hebrew Scripture into the Greek language took place in Africa. Furthermore, as Chaim Rabin of the Hebrew University in Jerusalem reminded the audience at the Jerusalem Congress on Black Africa and the Bible in April 1972, "There

75. Song, *Third-Eye Theology*, 123.
76. Levison and Pope-Levison, "Global Perspectives," 335.
77. Song, *Third-Eye Theology*, 141.

is no doubt that from the point of view of its structure and its ways of thinking, its directness, its imagery, the average African language is closer, a great deal closer, to Biblical Hebrew than the Biblical Hebrew is to any of the modern European languages."[78] Africa is closely bound to the Judeo-Christian religions and their sacred texts.

Christianity came to Africa by a circuitous route. Christianity appeared in Egypt and Roman North Africa in the first three centuries of the church's existence, well before Western Europe was Christianized. However, Christianity reached Africa south of the Sahara via Europeans when imperialist nations like Britain, France, and Germany came to be colonial powers on the continent of Africa. Christianity has been charged as an instrument employed by the European colonial powers to enslave and oppress the Africans. Many Africans have always viewed the Christian church as an imperialist agent: "the Christian missionary churches consciously aided the colonial powers in the enslavement and suppression of Africans."[79]

Majeke describes the role of missionaries as a process of peaceful penetration. Missionaries approached the chief humbly with a Bible in hand and asked for a small piece of land to set up a mission station. "The peaceful penetration by the missionary and the trader—sometimes the missionary turned trader—is followed in due course by an "agreement" between the chief and the Governor, whereby the British become the "friend and protector" of the chief. But this agreement" is actually the procursor of British interference, of war and the looting of cattle, and ends with a so-called "treaty in which the chief "agrees" to seizure of a large piece of land belonging to the tribe. In return he receives a magistrate as well as a missionary, who is much less humble than he was when he first arrived to beg land of the chief."[80] In due course, a land agreement between the chief and the governor would split, divide, and rule the tribes. Missionaries prepared the way for such activity by disarming the chiefs with their message of God's love and peace. They would often mediate negotiations between governors and the chiefs, acting frequently as the governor's advisors and assist in drawing up the

---

78. As quoted in Mbiti, "The Bible," 28.
79. Pobee, *Toward*, 15–16.
80. Majeke, *The Role of the Missionaries*, 6.

terms of the treaties. They become interpreters and peacemakers, while at the same time serving as advisors to the invaders.[81]

Since Christianity came to much of Africa via Europe, it came with European conditions, and so, in the African context, Christianity and they was taken to Africa by European colonizers in the context of imperialism. The African way of life was sabotaged by a European political, economic, social, and religious structure. In this context the method to interpret the meaning of the Bible was a western perspective. Therefore instead of attempting to glean the essence of the Bible with Western models of interpretation, the African theologian must replace the European methods with African methods of interpretation. "An analysis of disparate biblical interpretations yields what might be called a hermeneutic of resonance between Net Testament and traditional African culture." A "kindred atmosphere" is discerned in connecting traditional religion to that of the Hebrew Bible.[82]

The role of ancestors, who die physically but continue to live, resonates with the portrait of Jesus in the Gospel of John. Just as Jesus left his presence with the community, the ancestors provide a watchful presence over the community. The hermeneutic of resonance differs from the hermeneutic of liberation that characterizes the discussion among Black theologians in South Africa; while the hermeneutic of resonance draws resemblance with the similarities of ancestors and Jesus, the hermeneutic of liberation is about liberation from domination. Under the domination of apartheid, the paradigm of holistic liberation parallels the experience of South African Blacks that hoped to jettison White supremacy and regain access to their ancestral land.[83]

The term "African theology" is misleading because it gives the impression that one theology dominates the entire African continent, when in fact there are several different African theologies that are specific to the needs of particular countries and contexts. For the purposes of this section I will deal with a general African theology and a more specific South African black theology. African theology is the only theology that incorporates traditional African culture. It "is an inculturation theology whose goal is to integrate Christianity into the life and

---

81. Ibid., 5–7.
82. Levison and Pope-Levison, "Global Perspectives," 337.
83. Ibid., 337–39.

culture of African people." South African Black theology on the other hand, "relates the gospel message of liberation to its oppressive context of apartheid."[84]

Debates between African and South African Black theologies arise frequently between Manas Buthelezi, a South African theologian and Kwesi Dickson, an African theologian. Buthelezi often criticizes African theology for its ethnographic approach to theology. The emphasis on the traditional African worldview and culture neglects today's African person. He instead opts for an "anthropological theology that focuses on the person and the throbbing of life situations in which people find themselves." For Dickson, socioeconomic and political freedom is important, "but cultural freedom is essential for it defines, more fundamentally, the humanity of a people."[85]

Two hermeneutical options, therefore, characterize African biblical interpretations. A hermeneutic of resonance juxtaposes African traditional religion with the Bible and a South African hermeneutic of liberation emphasizes the current Black struggle.

Conclusion

In this chapter, I presented a new African meta-narrative of liberation by drawing from other oppressive contexts globally. What was explored was not a top-down model, nor a representation of scripture that supported oppressive narratives, but rather models that liberated and supported equality, humanity, dignity, and integrity the ubuntu way. I surveyed liberation theologies from three two-thirds world contexts—Asia, Latin American, Africa—looking for liberative trajectories in their hermeneutics that made sense of a Christian faith, which liberated humanity from oppressive narratives. The cumulative effect of the trajectories suggested by these theologies was to show that Biblical interpretation is incomplete without a global perspective. Although the Bible is context-specific and written to particular people, particular contexts, and particular times, it is only relevant today if it is contextualized for the readers' particular contexts.

Liberation theology is rooted in ones' experience. Liberating human beings from oppressive structures and reflecting on lived experi-

---

84. Pope-Levison and Levison, *Jesus in Global Contexts*, 92–93.
85. Ibid., 93.

ence is the primary source for doing theology with the use of social analysis for transforming social structures. This theology engages in its reflections and methodology within the people's life of faith and the struggles of oppressive living conditions. This influential methodology as the only way to do theology proper spread to other continents, "creating dialogue among theologians, church workers, political activists, educators, and students in North America, Africa, and Asia."[86]

The conversation between the various contexts surveyed in this chapter reveals shared sources and methods. These contextual theologies all begin with their own experiences, while engaging the Bible and Christian tradition as sources to incorporate a community in the theological process. Almost all contextual theologies begin with a pre-commitment to some specific experience, be it race, socioeconomic, culture, class, or gender. For feminist theologians it is women's experiences; for African-American and South African Black theology it is the Black experience; for African theologians it is cultural experience; for Latin American theologians, it is the experience of being poor and oppressed; for Asian theologians, it is the experience of poverty and religiosity.[87] The broader principles of liberation theology present the most developed method of social analysis for these various engagements with localized experiences. In each, the methodology carefully explores various levels of dependency. The dependency is two-fold: oppressed people face domination by internal classes and external foreign powers and corporations.

In contexts outside of Latin America, many theologians see the importance of social analysis, but they have not used it to the extent found in the liberation methodologies of their Latin American counterparts. Asian theologians adopt a selective Marxist social analysis, but are reluctant to utilize it fully because of its apparent western bias and its uncertain philosophical and economical base as illustrated in the collapse of the USSR. The same can be said for South African Black and African-American Black theologies. These theologies are more concerned with race issues and only peripherally with the class struggles that can be linked to capitalism and imperialism. Similarly, since African theology is more concerned about cultural issues, African theologians are often

---

86. Schubeck, *Liberation Ethics*, 6–8.
87. Pope-Levison and Levison, *Jesus in Global Contexts*, 175.

skeptical of the value of social analysis. I propose a combination of the cultural and social analyses is necessary to thoroughly dismantle the challenges of neo-colonialism and to establish a new African meta-narrative. For instance, liberation theology can incorporate social biographies of the urban poor, and in this way, one can learn more about the cultural aspect of the one's context which is a significant lack in current liberation methodology. This incorporation could complement social analysis and develop a more holistic liberation methodology.

All contextual theologies utilize Western Christian traditions. However, much caution must be exercised, since the past provides us with ample examples of its function as suppressing and controlling the oppressed. Slaves were taught to submit and obey passively since their reward was in heaven; women were and are still being barred from leadership positions. Colonized people were told they were pagan, and conversion required forsaking vestiges of their former culture. Therefore, some practitioners explored in this chapter removed themselves from oppressive legacies in order to harness their own traditions as liberating sources.

Individual reflection done in the comfortable settings of personal studies often results in academic theologians whose writings are irrelevant to specific contexts. Contextual theologians, by giving their communities prominent roles in the theological process, remind us that effective theologies are rarely individualized. As discussed earlier in this chapter, interpreters must always approach and analyze a text within its context and from their own context. There must be an ongoing dialogue to continue a tradition in spite of language and cultural changes. In a conversation with the text, an interpreter must become its partner in order to address the questions that arise from the interpreter's own political, economic, social, religious, and cultural contexts.

The model of interpretation that is presented in this chapter is that of a multiform conversation. On the one hand, interpreters are drawn to texts that address issues of their contexts. On the other hand, similar interests draw theologians to different texts. Liberation and African theologians, for example, share a common interest in the human significance of Jesus. However, they begin at different starting points. Liberation theologians start with the historical Jesus rather than the risen Christ. African theologians come to the Bible from a perspective to preserve communal cultural heritage; therefore, texts that emphasize

Jesus' membership in the universal human community are important. They emphasize the exemplary life Jesus lived, for in African traditional religions, humans achieve ancestral status by becoming exemplary humans.

To echo Robert McAfee Brown's words, every interpretation is a fusion of text and context; no one interpretation is universal. Therefore, the alternative reading of Romans 13 in Chapter 2 suits the South African meta-narrative of oppression and needed to be deconstructed since all theologies are contextually conditioned. It may take others to show us how conditioned, parochial, or ideologically captive our own theology is. Conversations must continue, even when they are unsettling. They can be life changing. We will explore some of these unsettling conversations in Chapter 4 by looking into stories told to the Truth and Reconciliation Commission after the fall of apartheid. Unsettling stories of love, hate, murder, detention, and kidnappings were confessed to the Commission. These stories were life changing to an entire country and demonstrate how ubuntu, though modeled in one nation, is an idea from which the whole world could learn.

4

Impact of a New Narrative

A Negotiated Settlement; Truth for Reconciliation

Introduction

UBUNTU, THE LIBERATING AFRICAN THEOLOGY, WHICH SUSTAINED the hope of the Black community through decades of oppression by White rule, was put into action within the processes of the Truth and Reconciliation Commission, where individual retributive justice was negotiated for restorative communal justice for the sake of reconciliation, national healing, and nation building. The impact of ubuntu provided a space for people to tell their stories of hate, love, murder, obedience, resistance, kidnapping, detention, corruption, deceit, confession, repentance, forgiveness, and reconciliation, for South Africans to listen to one another, and for the world to hear neglected narratives. The effects were a re-membering of a fragmented society and a joint struggle for a community to make sense of faith.

The question of how governments deal with human rights violations committed by former regimes is the focus of this chapter. South Africa's answer to this question has been the Truth and Reconciliation Commission (TRC), which was indeed an exemplary model and achieved its goal and purpose. The goal was to offer amnesty to perpetrators of apartheid crimes in exchange for the truth about the past in the full disclosure of their deeds to the victims. The purpose was to reconcile with former enemies, with the hope of bringing healing and reconciliation to the entire nation.

The TRC provided a safe place for people to tell their stories so that the whole nation and indeed the world could listen. The process provides a model for other countries facing similar issues. I draw conclusions on what lessons were learnt from these commissions and why the South African TRC remains an exemplary model for healing and reconciliation to the world. The TRC was a negotiated settlement between the outgoing Afrikaner National Party and the incoming African National Congress. To most Black South Africans it seemed that justice was being sacrificed for Christian mercy and this very well may have been the case for the ultimate achievement of ubuntu. While it may seem that offering amnesty to perpetrators and forgiving enemies denied the victims justice, the TRC embodied a different kind of justice.

This chapter examines a restorative justice that requires forgiveness for the sake of ubuntu. The South African commission's purpose was to bring about unity and reconciliation by providing a full disclosure of gross human rights violations committed in the past. It was based on the principle that reconciliation depends on forgiveness, and that forgiveness can only take place if gross violations of human rights are fully disclosed. The South African TRC remains the only alternative to Nuremberg, on the one hand, and amnesia, as in the case of the Armenian genocide, on the other. It charts a delicate course between the extremes of the justice model, as in Nuremburg, and that of the peace-at-all-costs model, as in Zimbabwe and Namibia. The TRC did not want to forget the past, but examine it with honesty and integrity. Once it had opened the past, it forgave. There could be no new, united, reconciled South Africa without a common acknowledgement of the past. South Africa's transition to democracy came at a price, a price that compromised justice for democracy. It was in fact a bargain with the enemy. To remember and forgive; ubuntu is the overarching meta-narrative of this chapter. This chapter provides examples of Commissions elsewhere and shows why South Africa's Truth and Reconciliation Commission was so successful.

Stories of Reconciliation

April 27, 1994 was a glorious day for me as a South African because it was the day South Africans had anxiously waited for many long years. The struggle against apartheid had been waged for this day. It was the day for which many had been detained, tortured, exiled, imprisoned, or brutally murdered. All South Africans could finally vote in a democratic election. Desmond Tutu was sixty-two years old and Nelson Mandela was seventy-six.

Reconciliation can only be satisfactorily achieved as the consequence of forgiveness. Without forgiveness from victims and repentance from perpetrators, reconciliation is stripped of its real power. It becomes only an idealistic concept for intellectual dialogue. Under Afrikaner Nationalism since 1910, South African people of color were controlled by the apartheid rule of H. Verwoerd, P. W. Botha, and F. W. de Klerk. South Africans since the 90s have encountered a new equally potent control, the spirit of Nelson Mandela and Desmond Tutu. Both men are icons of resistance against the apartheid era. One urges reconciliation while the other stresses forgiveness; both offer a new narrative in Africa.

Narratives are central to the African tradition. It allows traditions, philosophies, ideologies, customs, and theologies to be passed down from one generation to the next. Stories teach us to seek revenge and repayment, or to love, understand, forgive, reconcile, and see things through the eyes of another. Transforming stories such as the ones crafted by the lives of President Mandela and Bishop Tutu shape the future. "All of us come from different realities. For centuries, we have not shared each other's experiences. We are all searching for the truth. We don't know what the truth is. A part of this truth is that, until now, we cannot share each other's realities. We don't understand each other's sorrow and pain."[1] In the new atmosphere of reconciliation and nation building, victims and perpetrators of apartheid are finally given the opportunity to tell their stories.

No story is more moving than that of Nelson Mandela. After over 27 years of imprisonment for resisting apartheid, Mandela was released to become the first Black president of South Africa. This change occurred through neither a military coup nor a violent overthrow of the Afrikaner Nationalist Party; rather, it was brought about by means of amicable negotiations and compromise. F. W. de Klerk's government realized that they could no longer sustain their policies of apartheid, and Nelson Mandela and the African National Congress (ANC) decided for

---

1. These are the words of Wynand Malan, a member of South Africa's Truth and Reconciliation Commission, May 16, 1997, quoted in Smith, "A Nation," 20.

the best interests of the country to discontinue resistance in favor of a settlement.[2]

One of the pressing issues that dominated South African politics shortly after Mandela took office was the tragic legacy of apartheid. In 1993 at a conference in Kempton Park, Johannesburg, which extended from March to November, crucial negotiations took place between the political parties that laid the foundation for a new government. The adoption of an interim constitution was almost prevented by the National Party's demands for a blanket amnesty for political crimes and the ANC's refusal to compromise. The National Party sought a bill that would give total amnesty for past events without scrutiny by an independent commission. The ANC rejected this, but ended the stalemate by proposing that amnesty be included in the postscript of the interim constitution, with details to be worked out for a future democratically elected Parliament. Peace had been bought at the price of justice. This deal with the devil effectively precluded a satisfying justice. How then, could true reconciliation be hoped for?[3]

The interim constitution kept apartheid criminals from prosecution in the new democracy. The African concept, ubuntu, made popular by the teachings of Desmond Tutu, can be seen throughout the TRC process and was a strong sustaining force. Commitment to the principles of ubuntu helped the entire nation confront its past.[4]

"The ANC wanted a Truth Commission while the National Party favored a Reconciliation Commission. The former were concerned about the victims of apartheid, the latter were looking for amnesty for the perpetrators."[5] The ANC wanted an official investigation into the facts of human rights abuses. They had already launched two independent inquiries into human rights abuses perpetrated by their very own members in training camps in Angola. The results of these inquiries were not encouraging. They revealed crimes of torture and murder committed by ANC members. The ANC proposed an extensive inquiry into the atrocities committed by the apartheid government, hoping to

---

2. Muller-Fahrenholz, *The Art of Forgiveness*, 85.
3. Smith, 22.
4. Minow, "Between," 320.
5. Muller-Fahrenholz, *The Art of Forgiveness*, 85.

answer unresolved questions as well as honor victims.[6] The TRC was born in the negotiations between the political rivals of the ANC and the National Party. The final clause of the interim Constitution adopted in 1993 served as a bridge from a past plagued with division and separation to a future committed to human rights, democracy, and peaceful coexistence. On July 19, 1995 the parliament fulfilled this objective through the creation of a Truth and Reconciliation Commission.

In announcing the institution of the TRC, Justice Minister, Dullah Omar stated that each request for amnesty must accompany full and honest disclosures of the crimes in question. He added that a fundamental element of reconciliation in this process was that people know who committed what against whom. Omar himself had been the victim of poisoning by security agents. He asserted that reconciliation was not just a simple question of indemnity or amnesty, but it required people to come forward to confess their crimes, in order to be forgiven by their victims. Many, however, felt the TRC process was immoral and it encouraged exemption from punishment: "it was political power and impunity rather than national healing that were at stake."[7] How could anyone who had committed gross human rights violations be allowed to go free with only a confession and no expression of contrition or remorse?

Captain Jacques Hechter, who committed dozens of murders as a security policeman, appealed for amnesty. As he took the stand in Pretoria's City Council chambers to express contrition for the murders he committed, he read from a prepared text: "I believe that what I did was in the interests of the Republic of South Africa, my religion, and my Christian convictions. Today I am uncertain where I stand. I am sorry about the loss of lives. I hope this will result in reconciliation in South Africa."[8] In a subsequent interview David Goodman, a writer for the *Washington Quarterly*, inquired of Hechter if his apology was sincere and if he was truly sorry. Hechter responded, "Ach, I'm not fuckin' sorry for what I did. Look—I fought for my country, I believed in what I did, and I did a good job. They were my enemy at the time. That oke over there was a terr [a terrorist]," pointing to a Black activist waiting

---

6. Minow, "Between," 320.
7. Sipho, "Confess," 33.
8. Goodman, "Why," 176–77.

to testify whom Hechter had tortured with electric shock and beaten to the verge of death. "I gave him the hiding of his life he'll never forget. I did my job well and I'd do it again if the circumstances called for it. No, man, I am not really fuckin sorry for what I did."[9]

Any applicant applying for amnesty needed only to satisfy three main conditions according to the Promotion of National Unity and Reconciliation Act:

1) The act for which amnesty was required should have happened between 1960, the year of the Sharpeville massacre, and 1994, when President Mandela was inaugurated as the first democratically elected South African head of state. 2) The act must have been politically motivated. Perpetrators did not qualify for amnesty if they killed because of personal greed, but they did qualify if they committed the act in response to an order by, or on behalf of, a political organization such as the former apartheid state and its satellite Bantustan homelands, or a recognized liberation movement such as the ANC or PAC. 3) The applicant had to make a full disclosure of all the relevant facts relating to the offense for which amnesty was being sought. The rubric of proportionality had to be observed—that the means were proportional to the objective.[10]

While it seemed that justice was being sacrificed in that the miscreants of apartheid were in fact going unpunished. Nevertheless, they were forced to admit to their crimes on national television, exposing them to public humiliation, shame, and the judgment of the people. Many of the members of security forces who came forward were respectable members of their communities, whose actions were hidden from their peers. Often wives and children did not even know that their husbands or fathers were involved in such heinous crimes, or that they were members of death squads who regularly tortured and murdered detainees in their custody. This fact is clearly seen in a letter below from a radio team covering the TRC:

> My story begins in my late teenage years as a farm girl in the Bethlehem district of the Eastern Free State. As an eighteen-year-old, I met a young man in his twenties. He was working in a top security structure. It was the beginning of a beautiful

---

9. Ibid., 177.
10. Tutu, *No Future Without*, 49–50.

relationship. We even spoke about marriage. A bubbly, vivacious man who beamed out wild energy. Sharply intelligent. Even if he was an Englishman, he was popular with all the "Boere" Afrikaners. And all my girlfriends envied me. Then one day he said he was going on a "trip." "We won't see each other again ... maybe never again." I was torn to pieces. So was he. An extremely short marriage to someone else failed all because I married to forget. More than a year ago, I met my first love again through a good friend. I was to learn for the first time he had been operating overseas and that he was going to ask for amnesty. I can't explain the pain and bitterness in me when I saw what was left of that beautiful, big, strong person. He had only one desire-that the truth must come out. Amnesty didn't matter. It was only a means to the truth. A need to clean up. He was gruesomely plucked out of our lives at the beginning of the year. Was that the price he had to pay for what he believed in?

After my unsuccessful marriage, I met another policeman. Not quite my first love, but an exceptional person. Very special. Once again a bubbly, charming personality. Humorous, grumpy, everything in its time and place. Then he says: he and three of our friends have been promoted. "We're moving to a special unit. Now, now, my darling. We are real policeman now." We were ecstatic. We even celebrated. He and his friends would visit regularly. They even stayed over for long periods. Suddenly, at strange times, they would become restless. Abruptly mutter the feared word "trip" and drive off. I ... as a loved one ... knew no other life than of worry, sleeplessness, anxiety about his safety and where they could be. We simply had to be satisfied with: "What you don't know can't hurt you." And all that we as loved ones knew ... was what we saw with our own eyes. He became very quiet. Withdrawn. Sometimes he would just press his face into his hands and shake uncontrollably. I realized he was drinking too much. Instead of resting at night, he would wander from window to window. He tried to hide his wild, consuming fear, but I saw it. In the early hours of the morning between two and half past two, I jolt awake from his rushed breathing. Rolls this way, that side of the bed. He's pale. Ice cold in a sweltering night—sopping wet with sweat. Eyes bewildered, but dull like the dead. And the shakes. The terrible convulsions and blood-curdling shrieks of fear and pain from the bottom of his soul. Sometimes he sits motionless, just staring in front of him. I never understood. I never knew. Never realized what was being shoved down his throat during the "trips." I just went through hell. Praying, pleading: "God, what's happening? What's wrong with him? Could he have changed so much? Is he going mad? I can't handle the man anymore! But I can't get out. He's going to haunt me for the rest of my life if I leave him. Why, God?

Today I know the answers to all my questions and heartache. I know where everything began, the background. The role of "those at the top," the "cliques" and "our men" who simply had to carry out their bloody orders . . . like "vultures." And today they all wash their hands in innocence and resist the realities of the Truth Commission. Yes, I stand by my murderer who let me and the old White South Africa sleep peacefully. Warmly, while "those at the top" were again targeting the next "permanent removal from society" for the vultures.

I finally understand what the struggle was really about. I would have done the same had I been denied everything. If my life, that of my children and my parents was strangled with legislation. If I had to watch how White people became dissatisfied with the best and still wanted better and got it. I envy and respect the people of the struggle—at least their leaders have the guts to stand by their vultures, to recognize their sacrifices. What do we have? Our leaders are too holy and innocent. And faceless. I can understand if Mr. de Klerk says he didn't know, but dammit, there must be a clique, there must be someone out there who is still alive and who can give a face to "the orders from above" for all the operations. Dammit! What else can this abnormal life be other than a cruel human rights violation? Spiritual murder is more inhumane than a messy, physical murder. At least a murder victim rests. I wish I had the power to make these poor wasted people whole again. I wish I could wipe the old South Africa out of everyone's past. I end with a few lines that my wasted vulture said to me one night: "They can give me amnesty a thousand times. Even if God and everyone else forgive me a thousand times—I have to live with this hell. The problem is in my head, my conscience. There's only one way to be free of it. Blow my own brains out. Because that's where my hell is."[11]

Why Face The Past?

In April 1996, Nombwyselo Mhlawuli, a widow of one of the Cradock four murdered in the mid-eighties, urged the Commission to assist in the return of the hand severed from her husband's body at the time of

11. Ibid., 51–54.

his death. It is apparently preserved, pickled, in a bottle in Port Elizabeth. She wants it back for a proper burial; it would mark her husband's joining the ranks of the ordinary dead.[12]

Apartheid, an experiment in racial purity like Hitler's Nazism, is a failed ideology. The challenge to South Africa's newest democracy is to put something new in its place. "We must faithfully record the pain of the past so that a unified nation can call upon that past as a galvanizing force in the large tasks of reconstruction." At the height of the apartheid dictatorship, democracy, reconciliation, and national healing were good ideologies to dream about. Few dreamed that South African democracy might be so quickly negotiated, and settled. If reconciliation is the cement to ground solidarity, then it must be admitted that the old apartheid system was a mistake that resulted in deliberate evil. Apartheid was, in the words of Willem de Klerk, brother of the former President, "darkness masquerading as light."[13]

New governments of countries have faced demands of accountability for atrocities committed by previous domestic governments. Various solutions have been tried in attempts to come to terms with years of atrocities for which there is no conceivable recompense. Many Black leaders, even within the ANC wanted a proper form of justice for those who killed and repressed thousands of people of color under apartheid. Some advocated a tribunal similar to the one established in Nuremberg, Germany in 1945 to prosecute World War II war crimes.

The purpose of the South African Truth and Reconciliation Commission was to bring about unity and reconciliation through a full investigation and disclosure of gross human rights violations committed in the past. Its basis is the principle that reconciliation is dependent upon forgiveness, and that forgiveness can only take place if gross violations of human rights are fully disclosed.

There are still many factions in South Africa that have made it their business to denigrate, vilify, ridicule, and misrepresent the TRC's work. Those who benefited from apartheid saw the work of the Commission as a witch-hunt directed to that particular community and as an instrument to advance the political interests of the ANC. While others have vociferously claimed that the TRC has brought more damage to the

---

12. Asmal, *Reconciliation Through Truth*, 146.
13. Ibid.

country than reconciliation. They assert that the TRC has "engendered resentment and anger, opened old wounds, and fostered alienation." To these claims, Tutu responds that his experience with the TRC has been the direct opposite. "It has been breathtaking, this willingness to forgive, this magnanimity, this nobility of spirit."[14]

Psychological Aspects of the TRC in South Africa

The mother's voice cracked with the unbearable agony: "I found Bheki. He was in pieces. He was hanging on the curtains, he was all over, there were pieces of brains all over. That was the end of Bheki." Catherine Mlangeni tells the story of the murder of her son Bheki Mlangeni. Next to her sits the daughter-in-law Sepati, listening, crying, remembering. Bheki, a promising young Soweto lawyer, was blown to pieces by a booby-trapped tape player headset. Archbishop Tutu vicariously wipes a tear on behalf of the nation.[15]

The work of the TRC was based on the final clause of the Interim Constitution, which reads as follows:

> This Constitution provides a historic bridge between the past of a deeply divided society characterized by strife, conflict, untold suffering, and injustice, and a future founded on the recognition of human rights, democracy and peaceful co-existence and development of opportunities for all South Africans, irrespective of color, race, class, belief or sex.
>
> The pursuit of national unity, the well-being of all South African citizens and peace require reconciliation between the people of South Africa and the reconstruction of society.
>
> The adoption of this constitution lays the secure foundation for the people of South Africa to transcend the divisions and strife of the past, which generated gross violations of human rights, the transgression of humanitarian principles in violent conflicts, and a legacy of hatred, fear, guilt, and revenge. These can now be addressed on the basis that there is a need for understanding but not for vengeance, a need for reparation but not retaliation, a need for ubuntu but not for victimization.
>
> In order to advance such reconciliation and reconstruction, amnesty shall be granted in respect of acts, omissions and offences associated with political objectives and committed in

---

14. Tutu, "Between," 25.
15. Dowdall, "Theological," 9.

the course of the conflicts of the past. To this end, Parliament under this Constitution shall adopt a law determining a firm cut-off date which shall be a date after October 8, 1990 and before December 1993, and providing for the mechanisms, criteria and procedures, including tribunals, if any, through which such amnesty shall be dealt with at any time after the law has been passed.

With this Constitution and these commitments we, the people of South Africa, open a new chapter in the history of our Country.[16]

If Justice Minister Omar had gone to Parliament and produced an amnesty law, he would have ignored the victims. He recognized that unless attempts to restore the honor and dignity of the victims were made, the forgiveness of the perpetrators could not take place. There was a dire need for both individual and collective healing to take place. This healing was necessary for building a nation that guaranteed peace and stability.

Regardless of the angle from which one views the work of the TRC in South Africa, it is evident that at its heart exists the need for psychological transformation. It is important to note that the focus of the TRC against the "evils of apartheid" in South Africa is also part of a much larger worldwide struggle. The use of violent repression, murder, and torture, to enforce state policy is, "no longer respected as the private domestic concern of states, just as wife-battering and child abuse is no longer regarded as the private domestic business of the family."[17]

Following the Nuremberg trials and other Truth commissions, the international community has monitored authoritarian governments involved in atrocities of gross human rights abuse. The work of the TRC affirms the international consensus by saying "no" to violent repression by police, politicians, and soldiers.

One of the problems that most commissions have to deal with is the question of impunity, "a blanket absolution and protection for those who committed horrific crimes in the line of duty."[18] Crimes are often concealed, rather than condemned, by the governing authorities. In a

---

16. Omar, "Introduction," 24–25. For full text of the interim constitution see http://www.servat.unibe.ch/icl/sf10000_.html.
17. Dowdall, "Theological," 29.
18. Ibid.

way, the governments condone these acts of torture, rape, and murder. Impunity is not to admit, to apologize for, or to be prosecuted for these crimes against humanity.[19]

The TRC strove to find a delicate balance in dealing with the question of impunity without imperiling reconciliation. It had no intentions to begin a witch-hunt against perpetrators, yet it was imperative to send out a message that no end will justify gross human rights violations. Minister of Justice Omar made this clear when he said, "the objective of the exercise is not to conduct a witch-hunt or to drag violators of human rights before court to face charges . . . but that a commission is a necessary exercise to enable South Africans to come to terms with their past on a morally accepted basis and to advance the cause of reconciliation."[20]

However, many White South Africans saw the TRC as just that, a witch-hunt by the ANC. White critics further said that the ANC was equally involved in crimes against apartheid, and that little attention was being given to that issue. While credence must be given to this accusation, the ANC's scattered infringements committed by those resisting apartheid were but only aberrations that cannot be compared with the wholesale atrocities of apartheid. The ANC did not single out any apartheid leader for assassination, while the Apartheid State systematically targeted its opponents. The anti-apartheid resistance consisted of citizens uniting in self-defense while the apartheid regime presided over the state and abused their responsibilities.[21]

While South Africa's bargain with evil was necessary in order for elections, a peaceful transition to democracy, and efforts to reconcile a broken nation, the kind of justice that the majority of the Blacks were seeking was not the kind of justice that would move the country ahead toward the building and healing of the nation. Many Blacks viewed the negotiations with the former oppressors as one of the weaknesses of the TRC. However, through the public nature of its hearings and its intrinsic moral force, the TRC played an important role in the restoration of respect for right and wrong in South Africa.[22]

19. Ibid., 28–30.
20. Omar, "Introduction," 26.
21. Asmal, *Reconciliation Through Truth*, 7.
22. Dowdall, "Theological," 28–29.

In many repressive states around the globe, the state constructs for itself a romanticized picture of a guardian that protects its citizens from barbarians. This portrait was clearly epitomized during the apartheid era among White South Africans who viewed and treated people of color as barbarians. Former President F. W. de Klerk went so far as to state that apartheid was a good intention that failed. Yet, to most, it seems obvious that apartheid was a system constructed to dehumanize and deny people of color respect and dignity while allowing White privilege. By giving space to the stories of human rights victims, the Commission plays an important role in exposing these romanticized notions, which are in reality horrific and shameful actions of perpetrators. It contributes to the rehabilitation of the victim by breaking through the culture of silence. Since stress, anxiety, and depression commonly result from suppressing or repressing painful memories, the process of revealing these painful stories in a supportive and affirming setting often brings healing. It serves as a catharsis to the nation as a whole.[23]

It was a clear conviction of the TRC that only by examining past injustice was it possible for the nation to forge ahead in a manner of integrity and profundity. However, the question in the minds of many concerned the seemingly irreconcilable objectives of the TRC in its vision to provide dignity for the victims and amnesty for the perpetrators. Many wondered whether the process of painful remembering would lead to mutual understanding or renewed hatred.

Eugene de Kock was in charge of a Special Forces Unit whose operations base was a solitary farm called Vlakplaas. From Vlakplass he and his men committed assassinations and massacres all over Southern Africa with the knowledge and support of leaders in top positions. When de Kock applied for amnesty the people could not help but question whether such atrocities could ever be forgiven. Such questioning, anger, sadness, grief, and shock resonated in South Africa at the beginning of healing process. The work of the TRC has been cathartic. Ironically, victims during detention and torture were told: "Yell as loud as you wish; nobody will ever hear you." Now, the nation heard; the whole world heard. The torturers who were once beyond reproach were being named. As men and women recall their memories and face their pain in public, they face their anguish and suffering, thus, beginning the

---

23. Ibid., 32.

healing process. This is the beginning of renewed dignity. A correction of history restores the humiliated.[24]

The TRC as a Ritual for Healing in South Africa

> There was the White woman victim who was attacked on a golf course. She was so badly injured her children had to teach her to do things we take for granted. She still can't go through security check points at airports because she has so much shrapnel in her body. She said, "I would like to meet the perpetrator in a spirit of forgiveness." That's wonderful! She goes, "I would like to forgive him," and then quite incredibly she adds, "and I hope he will forgive me." Crazy.
>
> Then there was the Afrikaner father whose toddler son was killed in the ANC Amanzimtoti Wimpy Bar bomb attack. He said, "he believed his son had contributed to the coming of the new dispensation;" or the Afrikaner woman in Klerksdorp who testified about the abduction of her husband by liberation army operatives and said, her grief and loss were just a drop in the ocean compared to what other people have suffered in this beautiful traumatized land; or the daughter who, after hearing all the gruesome details of how her father had been killed, said, "We would like to forgive, we just want to know whom to forgive." Incredible.
>
> —Desmond Tutu[25]

South Africa was host to one of the most valid amnesty processes in history. In the words of Archbishop Tutu, whom President Nelson Mandela elected to head the TRC, "Nobody was in a position to enforce so-called victor's justice. Without some amnesty provisions our reasonably peaceful transition from repression to democracy would instead have become a bloodbath."[26] The South African TRC consisted of three committees. It operated for a period of almost two and a half years. It consisted of a Human Rights Violations Committee, an Amnesty Committee, and a Reparations and Rehabilitation Committee. It operated with a budget of $18 million, per year, several million more than

---

24. Muller-Fahrenholz, *The Art of Forgiveness*, 88–89.
25. Tutu, "Between a Nightmare and a Dream," 25–26.
26. As quoted in Torrens, "The Many," 16.

the budget of commissions in countries like Chile ($1 million) and El Salvador ($2.5 million).[27]

The proceedings of the TRC were distinctive in several ways. The TRC conducted much of its work in open forums open to international media, unlike some Latin American commissions, which were held behind closed doors. The TRC's proceedings began with victims coming forward and telling their stories. Of the twenty thousand applicants, only ten percent were accommodated in public hearings, while staff members heard the rest. Sixteen hundred applications for amnesty were received by the TRC and while amnesty was granted in over half of the cases, there were clear exceptions. In one of the most emotionally charged cases, the TRC denied amnesty to the two men who had assassinated Chris Hani, leader of the Communist Party and likely successor to President Nelson Mandela. The men who were responsible for Hani's death failed to tell the whole truth and acted without the endorsement of their political party.[28]

As the present work hopes to demonstrate, the very institution of a TRC in South Africa can be seen as an overarching ubuntu ritual of healing. At the same time, one ought to note how the nation participated in more specific and concrete rituals during the TRC process. These too, contributed to the ubuntu ideals. For instance, reporting the work of the TRC on television became ritualistic for reporter and viewers alike. Even with TRC's small media budget, its work dominated South African television. Whether it was clips of Robben Island where Nelson Mandela and many other political activists were incarcerated or a hearing at a remote town of Ladybrand, the effects of the TRC monopolized the eight o'clock news night after night. Journalist and poet Antjie Krog spoke of the ubiquitous TRC microphone as having become the symbol of the Commission: "It guarantees the access of the marginalized voice to the public ear. The translation of the unspeakable, the words and the voice of the unformulateable."[29] The microphone, in an uncanny way, symbolized the innermost depths of each individual story while simultaneously connecting the nation to the collective revelations and memories of lost ones.

27. Torrens, "The Many," 16.
28. Torrens, "The Many," 15.
29. Krog, "The Truth," 7–8.

The choices of the towns and venues in which hearings would take place were also critical issues for the Commission to consider in its early stages. These decisions, too, demonstrate the ubuntu ideology that permeated the TRC's activities. The first TRC hearings took place in East London, a city in the Eastern Cape, which was known for its aggressive anti-apartheid activists. During the enforced State of Emergency by the government, Blacks were randomly stopped at checkpoints and had their cars searched. Materials found that the police deemed "suspicious," were enough ample reason for beatings and detention. Detention could be a weekend, several months or years. It was common for families not to know the whereabouts of their loved ones. Curfews were imposed for Blacks to leave White cities by a certain time. If the police suspected people of political involvement they could be subjected to random house searches, which more often than not resulted in imprisonment. During the 80s forty percent of all detainees in the whole country came from East London.[30] The TRC made a bold reconciliatory decision by holding the first hearings here.

The selection of venue was a decision of significance as well. "By choosing the city hall and not several centers in the township ... the Commission gave notice of its determination to perform the ritual of claiming space, of consecrating a space, indicating that this once belonged to Whites, now it belongs to all of us."[31] The commission announced its occupancy of the city hall by means of banners and posters and not without police security. Ironically, many of the officers who stood at the doors now protected the very victims they once victimized. Their presence now symbolized that they were making the space safe so that victims could come and tell their stories.

Public services were usually held on the Sundays before a hearing started. The services symbolized the ideas of ubuntu for many South Africans. Desmond Tutu became the keynote speaker for most of the services, which always drew large crowds, including many victims and their relatives. These services often included ritualistic symbols. In East London, inside of a church, a fire was lit in a wheelbarrow for the families of victims. The venue where the hearings took place were acknowledged as sacred space separated from the rest of the audience and even

---

30. Krog, "The Truth," 7–10.
31. Ibid., 9.

from the commissioners themselves. Services contained reverential markers such as the Candle, the Litany for the Dead, and the Silence of Remembrance. While everyone stood, the Candle was lit and the names of the victims and the dead were read. This was followed by a moment of silence. The hearing then opened with scripture, a song, or a spoken or silent prayer.[32]

The ritual of releasing or exorcising terrible memories occurred in the victims' telling of their stories. These stories employed neither overly ornate language nor subtleties. They were harsh, unadorned stories about brutality, cruelty, and senseless hurt and destruction. Through the TRC, the people of South Africa were able to utilize words and stories to come to grips with the past. They were given an opportunity to live through their individual stories and shared meta-narratives. To one, a narrative of love was expressed; to another, it was a narrative of pain, heartache, and bitter memories. We communicate, confess, forgive, and reconcile through our meta-narratives. We participate in each other's humanity in the form of meta-narratives to express our common narratives of pain, suffering, loss, and anguish that apartheid caused.[33]

The question, however, as to whether the TRC was a ritual for healing of the nation is a difficult one. It certainly had the potential for this, but it is difficult to measure the full measure of the healing because a significant part of the White South African community ignored the Commission and did not participate in its activity. Many Afrikaners justified their lack of participation by claiming that the TRC existed solely for the Black victims and their White perpetrators. One wonders though, if it could have been deep shame that caused them to avoid direct confrontation with the horrendous facts. Or could it be denial that these atrocities really did not take place? When people suffer the effects of shame, excuses multiply. "Barricades of innocence and indifference are erected: We did not do it! We did not know of it! At least we did not want it to be done this way!"[34] Desensitization often takes place when people are confronted with truths of horror. For truth does not only liberate, but can also numb the conscience. When faced with the truth of extreme guilt, people need to be comforted and accepted. Within South

32. Krog, "Parable," 7–11.
33. Botman and Peterson, *To Remember and to Heal*, 37.
34. Muller-Fahrenholz, *The Art of Forgiveness*, 89.

African society, many Whites seemed unable to fathom or desire the possibility that they might be held and comforted by Blacks.[35]

In the words of Tutu, "those who deride the TRC hardly ever refer to an amazing phenomenon—the victim's readiness, indeed eagerness, to forgive. Many are seemingly taking it for granted—as something almost to which they are entitled."[36] South Africa is fortunate in the sense that the country has not found peace devastatingly elusive, as it has been for Angola, Sudan, Bosnia, Northern Ireland, Sri Lanka, India, Kashmir, Pakistan, and parts of the Middle East. Blacks still arise from their poverty-stricken settlements in the early morning to travel to the affluent suburbs of their White employers. At night, they return to their unlit homes of squalor. "They actually go back to all that and don't go on a rampage in the largely White pockets of comfort and affluence. Yet, all some Whites do is moan about their loss of power."[37] Black analysts speak of the "boss-client relationship." They suggest that many White people are entrenched in this mentality to such a degree that it sincerely does not cross their minds to expect help from or to owe something to those that they consider inferiors. Sadly, it is still the case in South Africa that many Whites perceive people of color as inferior. It is difficult to fathom that while Blacks express their willingness to forgive, Whites consider it normal, since the *baas* (boss) had no reason to ask his or her servants for forgiveness.[38]

"Let bygones be bygones," represents an attitude held by many Whites that cannot be embraced by Black Africans. This attitude, typical of many Western Europeans, regards the past as over and finished. Black Africans view the past differently. For example, Europeans do not honor the dead in the same way that Africans do. Africans feel that the spirits of the dead are still with them and that it is vitally important to reconcile with unredeemed spirits of the past. This is deeply rooted in ubuntu spirituality. This spirituality cannot be dismissed as naïve or pagan, but it is to be recognized as a worldview very much in touch with the fundamental connectedness of all life. For Africans, the past is more than a matter of settling legal claims; it is an act of remembering, of

---

35. Ibid., 89–90.
36. Tutu, "Between a Nightmare and a Dream," 26.
37. Tutu, "Between a Nightmare and a Dream," 26.
38. Muller-Fahrenholz, *The Art of Forgiveness*, 90–93.

bringing back together what belongs together. It has to do with healing, redemption, reconciliation, and liberation. Ubuntu, the connectedness of all human beings, transcends the violent mechanisms of denial and retaliation that characterizes White western culture.[39]

Can White South Africans see the TRC as an opportunity to begin to understand and perhaps even benefit from the rich spirituality of their Black fellow citizens? Can they grasp the victims' readiness to forgive them as an opportunity for them to flee their prisons of shame and dungeons of denial? With the spirit of ubuntu, Desmond Tutu hopes so:

> I am as committed to White liberation as I am to Black liberation. Whites won't be free until we are free . . . We won a victory for everyone, Black and White. Now we have all been liberated. Freedom is indivisible. Come share in the process of healing, in the process of reconciliation . . . Reconciliation is a national project. We should all be involved . . . Get out of your ghetto of self-pity, of not acknowledging how lucky we all are.[40]

Conclusions

> Three burly Afrikaners walk in, ex-security police whose vicious rule once ran throughout South Africa. One of them reads from a prepared text: We blindfolded them and took them to a stone quarry outside the town. We hung Subject Number 1 upside down from a tree branch and lit a fire under him. When his hair burned he screamed a lot and then he told us everything. The other two also confessed. After that, we shot them. Our report said they had resisted arrest.[41]

In this chapter I focused on one question: How do governments deal with human rights violations committed by former oppressive regimes? South Africa's answer to that question was found in the spirit of ubuntu operating in the processes of the TRC. The goal of the TRC was to offer amnesty to perpetrators of apartheid crimes in exchange for the truth about the past in the full disclosure of their deeds to the victims. The purpose was to reconcile with former enemies in hopes that ubuntu

39. Ibid., 92–93.
40. Tutu, "Between a Nightmare and a Dream," 26.
41. Storey, "A Different Kind," 788.

would bring healing to the entire nation. I noted other countries' use of Truth Commissions and highlighted what lessons South Africa learnt and mistakes it avoided. I provided reasons why South Africa's TRC remains one of the more successful commissions to date. Even though the TRC was a negotiated settlement between the outgoing Afrikaner National Party and the incoming African National Congress in the transition from totalitarianism to democracy, to many it seemed that justice was being sacrificed for Christian mercy. However, the ultimate goal was the achievement of ubuntu. Since offering amnesty to perpetrators and forgiving enemies denied the victims a traditional form of justice, I offered examples of the TRC embodying a different kind of justice hinting to restorative justice requiring forgiveness for the sake of ubuntu as the overarching meta-narrative of this chapter. The impact of ubuntu, provided a space, a forum, a place for people to come tell their narratives, stories of hate, love, murder, obedience, resistance, kidnapping, detention, corruption, deceit, confession, repentance, forgiveness, and reconciliation were all told for South Africa to hear, for the world to listen, for a re-membering back into one society, a community struggling to make sense of faith.

A different kind of confession took place during South Africa's Truth and Reconciliation Commission—different in that the confessing was not to bring judgment to the confessor, but healing and reconciliation to wounded beings. This time Ubuntu one being human is contingent and deeply connected to the other being humanook precedence as an inclusive sense of community valuing everyone. This time "inferior" Black Africans attempted to show the "superior" past regime a different way of dealing with the crimes of the past. Inspired by Nelson Mandela and Desmond Tutu, South Africans have shown an extraordinary willingness to confront the demons of the past in an effort to bring about peace, reconciliation, and stability. In this confessional process, perpetrators started their personal journeys of healing and recovery by having a safe platform to talk publicly about their sinful deeds, and victims were given a place to recount the effects of the oppressive narrative and offer forgiveness to their persecutors, all of which began the process of reconciliation between individuals and the nation. The TRC was not perfect. It was a compromise between two political parties, but it did provide a workable model to nations moving through democratic transitions in its ethical and pragmatic experimentation in dealing with the past.

The Commission drew worldwide attention for the methods employed in dealing with the brutality of apartheid. It proved to be an exercise like no other in history. It gave equal priority to both victims and perpetrators in the confessional process. However, South Africa's transition to democracy came at a price, a price that did in fact compromise justice for democracy. It was in fact a bargain, a negotiated settlement with the National party and the ANC. Some would have liked justice, punishment, imprisonment, and the death penalty for perpetrators, but that may not have achieved the amicable results of reconciliation, healing, and nation building that President Mandela sought. South Africa would not have been a model to the rest of the world and would not have been involved in negotiating peace talks around the globe as they have since the successful transition to democracy in 1994.

There could be no new, united South Africa without a common acknowledgement of the past. This required considerable courage and honesty in confronting the brutal oppression of the apartheid years. Other commissions and investigations in Germany, Philippines, and Latin America offered more warnings than guidance. The Nuremberg trials dispensed harsh retribution to the top echelon of Nazi criminals but ignored their victims and allowed ordinary Germans to continue to live in a state of denial. In Chile and Argentina, the army and police made general confessions in exchange for blanket amnesty, which permitted the perpetrators to evade personal accountability. There the mothers of the "disappeared ones" were denied justice.

How successful was the TRC process in South Africa? Tales of torture, police brutality, and detention without trial, township raids, and bombs exploding in downtown centers had been revealed by thousands of people of various ethnicities and political parties. While it was a cathartic experience, these individuals will never see justice, for the perpetrators were given amnesty. How does any state compensate for the loss of a loved one? While the Commission may have accomplished its goal of revealing the truth of the apartheid regime, the goal of reconciliation is an ongoing process and maybe harder to achieve in all instances. When Brian Mitchell, a young White policeman who received amnesty for planning the massacre of eleven Zulu women and children, went back to the community to offer his service, he was not readily accepted.⁴² Reconciliation without truth is impossible, but truth does not necessarily lead to reconciliation. Forgiveness needs to take place before reconciliation can happen. The TRC can be seen as only the starting point of a process. Reconciliation and the ubuntu that Tutu talks about might take South Africa a lifetime to accomplish, given its tragic past. However, with the model given to us by reconciliatory leaders such as Desmond Tutu and Nelson Mandela, the possibility of ubuntu for the ordinary citizen becomes easier to imagine.

Weaknesses of the TRC

Amnesty has been the most controversial topic of the TRC process. The families of Steve Biko, a young man who started the Black consciousness movement and was murdered in 1977, Griffiths Mxenge, a lawyer brutally stabbed to death by police in 1981, and Chris Hani, who was assassinated on the eve of the South African elections, opposed applications for amnesty from the perpetrators. In these cases victims and their families wanted true justice for the crimes of apartheid, and amnesty was not to be part of the negotiation package.

Because the TRC focused on the bloody and gruesome activities of the "foot soldiers" who typically carried out instructions from the top, one might consider it a shortcoming of the Commission that it was hindered from exposing the planners and top officials of apartheid who actually gave the orders. A second weakness is that the TRC did not require the perpetrators to demonstrate remorse or show any willingness to make reparations for their actions. All that was needed was a full disclosure of the truth. With this, the Commission granted amnesty to the perpetrators. A third and related weakness is that the TRC demonstrated less concern for reparations to the victims. Some view this as a tip of the scales in favor of the perpetrators. It is further asserted that the TRC would grant victims opportunities to relate their stories, in order that measures aimed at reparation, rehabilitation, and restoration may take place. However relating one's story may not be enough. Perpetrators are given amnesty, while victims do not receive justice. Instead, they get their stories recorded.⁴³

---

42. Tutu, *No Future Without Forgiveness*, 176–77.
43. Maluleke, "Truth," 66–67.

Any attempt to address the past must surely acknowledge the suffering of people in the apartheid system. To aid reconciliation one has to take into account the cries of both those who demanded "prosecute and punish," and those who insisted on "forgive and forget." The Rustenburg declaration was perhaps the first sign that healing was necessary in order for any transition to occur within South Africa. The birth of the TRC was aided by this remarkable church conference held in Rustenburg in 1990. Both churches that opposed and supported apartheid released a common confession of sin.

Unique Features of the TRC

The TRC in South Africa was characterized by a number of unique factors not found in Commissions elsewhere. The TRC originally and ideally set out to give priority to the victims rather than the perpetrators. In the words of Father Michael Lapsley who was partially blinded and maimed by a parcel bomb in the guise of a religious magazine from the security forces, "this committee must ensure that people's suffering is heard, recognized and reverenced by the nation."[44]

Another unique aspect of the TRC was that the victims from all sides of the struggle participated. Those who suffered at the hands of the liberation forces were also invited to share their experiences. A story of a secret police torture might have been followed by a White farmer's story of how his wife and children were killed by an ANC land mine. "A morally justified struggle does not justify indiscriminate killing and deliberate brutality."[45] This fact is seen in the notoriously violent actions of the anti-apartheid revolutionary group, Pan African Congress (PAC), who engineered the murder of American exchange student, Amy Biehl, simply because she was White in a Black township. The parents of Amy Biehl were able to walk into the venue of the hearings to confront the murderers of their daughter. "Has it been too neatly choreographed for public consumption?" asks Joyce Hollyday, writer for the Sojourners Magazine. Hollyday questions, "Why is it that the world pays so much attention to the murder of an American while the deaths of thousands of South Africans remain tucked away on the back pages of history?"[46]

44. Storey, "A Different Kind," 789.
45. Ibid., 790.
46. Hollyday, "Hearts," 2.

Many South Africans wonder if they should be expected to forgive police officers and doctors who collaborated in the brutal murder of Steve Biko or Chris Hani. The point is that the TRC was impartial to any one group and refused to exempt the anti-apartheid movements such as the ANC or PAC from coming before the Commission and confessing their crimes. This is evidenced in the intensive hearings related to the activities of Winnie Mandela who was at that time the wife of the first Black president. The TRC further subpoenaed Former State President P. W. Botha to a court of law for his failure to appear before the Commission.[47]

A monumental opportunity for healing and forgiveness was lost when P. W. Botha refused to acknowledge either the TRC or his own reign of terror. This was in spite of the fact that the TRC had discovered that almost eighty percent of all cases of human rights violations and amnesty cases came between 1984 and 1990, the years when Botha was president.[48] More disappointing was the symbolic testimony of F. W. de Klerk, who apologized in general but refused to admit knowledge of the work of the security forces. In an interview with Bill Moyers, US journalist, Max Du Prez covering the TRC reflects, "I think that one of the biggest disappointments of this whole process was when . . . De Klerk said, 'I acknowledge now that these things happened, but I did not know at the time, and I certainly did not order it.' and that's not true . . . I personally told him about the police death squads in 1989."[49]

The responses of Botha and de Klerk echoed revelations made in speeches from the Nuremberg trials. President Richard Freiherr von Weizsacher of the Republic of Germany impressed the world with his, "unflinching, excuseless enumeration of Nazi crimes and many degrees of association with those crimes by millions of Germans in the years 1933–45. It was believed to be the first time a senior West German leader publicly challenged the widely heard justification that ordinary Germans were unaware of the Holocaust."[50] In concluding his denunciation he stated,

---

47. Hollyday, "Hearts," 2.
48. Jones, "Truth," 60.
49. Ibid., 61.
50. Shriver, *An Ethic for Enemies*, 108.

> To implement his unfathomable hatred ... Hitler had never kept it from the public, but rather made the entire nation the tool of this hatred. It was a crime without historical precedent. Though much of the gruesome operation was in fact shielded from the eyes of the public, it was still true that every German could witness what Jewish fellow citizens had to suffer, from cold indifference through veiled intolerance to open hatred. Who could remain innocent after the burning of the synagogues, the looting, the stigmatizing with the Jewish star, the withdrawal of rights, the unceasing violations of human worth?
>
> Whoever opened his eyes and ears, whoever wanted to inform himself, could not escape knowing that deportation trains were rolling. All of us, whether guilty or not, whether old or young, must accept the past. We must accept it by remembering it and never forgetting it.
>
> Whoever closes his eyes to the past becomes blind to the present. Whoever does not wish to remember inhumanity becomes susceptible to the dangers of new infection. As human beings, we seek reconciliation. Precisely for this reason we must understand that there can be no reconciliation without memory.[51]

As the TRC proceeded with its task, hardened Whites dismissed the process with angry denials and referred to it as the "Kleenex Commission." They questioned the validity of these stories in the absence of a cross-examination procedure, but the cumulative effect of hundreds of stories of horror and pain changed the mood of the country as the TRC continued. Denial became defensiveness, which then started the process of corporate shame. Victims indeed seem to have benefited through the process, since the overwhelming sentiment of victims is that they now feel able to go forward with their lives.[52]

The leadership of Archbishop Desmond Tutu also distinguished the TRC. He wept with victims and marked every moment of repentance and forgiveness. He did not hesitate to reflect theologically throughout the process. Justice Albie Sachs, a White South African and anti-apartheid activist lost an arm and suffered other injuries when an Afrikaner bomb went off in his car, is now judge of the South African Constitutional Court. Sachs notes that, "Tutu cries. A judge does not cry," alluding to the humanness brought to a process that was administered

---

51. Ibid., 109–10.
52. Storey, "A Different Kind," 798.

in a court like fashion.⁵³ The leadership of Tutu and other clergy on the commission provided a safe place for the victims and perpetrators.

Reconciliation and Jutstice

Reconciliation is difficult to achieve even when the truth is told. The TRC had uncovered the truth in a very powerful way with confession. While the TRC's efforts at times yielded reconciliation between victims and perpetrators, there were situations where reconciliation proved difficult and impossible. This was especially prevalent in cases in which the truth was told without any expression of remorse or repentance. As one White South African described, "How can I apologize for an act of war? War is war."[54] How long will "anti-communism" and "anti-terrorism" serve as pretexts for waging war on innocent people and excusing heinous injustices? How long will these unsupportable rationales mask the real terrorism perpetrated by police and military authorities?

South African feminist theologian Denise Ackermann relays a powerful story about a man named Bernie. Bernie joined the army upon his completion of high school. After his basic training, he was called to the border. The border was soon crossed, and he was moved into action in Angola. This experience changed his life forever. Because actions across the border were not just for protecting it from trespassers but included covert operations of kidnapping, torture, and murder of exiles and political activists. When Bernie returned home, he suffered nightmares, insomnia, and depression. He sought to reduce his pain in many ways. Fifteen months after his third attempt at marriage, he committed suicide. Bernie is one of many White young men who, "were lied to by their leaders, a tool in an evil system. I mourn for Bernie. He was my son-in-law."[55]

Poet Antjie Krog, tells a parable about a bicycle:

> There was Tom and there was John. One day, Tom stole John's bicycle and every day John saw Tom cycling to school on his bicycle. A year later, Tom walked up to John. He stretched out his hand. 'Let's reconcile and put the past behind us.' John looked at

---

53. Minow, "Between," 335.
54. Jones, "Truth," 61.
55. Ackermann, "On Hearing," 55–56.

Tom's hand. 'And what about the bicycle?' 'No,' said Tom, 'I'm not talking about the bicycle. I'm talking about reconciliation.'"[56]

The anecdote summarizes South Africa's past. President Mandela asked his people to forget about the bicycle and talk about reconciliation. His people listened, stretched out their hands and embraced the idea for unity, equality, plurality, and a reconciled healed nation. The TRC was a start. In contrast, the United States still wrestles with issues of injustice and racism toward African Americans, Hispanics, and other immigrant groups. America, the melting pot of cultures and colors, has not had president of color yet. South Africa's democracy is only 13 years old, with their second Black president. Reconciliation will take time but at least the TRC has put them on a positive and healthy track for national healing.

So what about the justice in the truth process? According to Tutu, "there does exist an 'eye for an eye,' type of justice. But at the same time there is another kind of justice, restorative justice, which requires forgiveness . . . forgiveness is no nebulous spiritual thing that is practiced by those who are crazy and idealistic and totally not pragmatic. Forgiveness is a pragmatic absolute necessity. Without forgiveness, there is no future. That is not a religious statement—it is thoroughly political. It is realpolitik."[57]

Who would have thought that South Africa could be held as a paradigm, as a model for anything other than that of Afrikaner barbarianism? The outgoing National Party reluctant to lose control and afraid of losing power bargained with the ANC. The ANC, wanting not only power to control but also freedom and equality in the spirit of ubuntu for all, negotiated, giving amnesty to the perpetrators in exchange for the truth. The result was a peaceful transfer to a fully democratic society—a settlement negotiated.

56. Krog, "Parable," 1.
57. Goodman, "Why," 178.

5

From Apartheid's Christian Hegemony to Religious Pluralism

Introduction

> One day while the Buddhist nun was chanting, beating her drum which apparently annoyed the parliamentarians, and holding her vigil which apparently annoyed the police, I stood watching the responses of pedestrians passing on Government Avenue. Some stopped, some passed, some gathered around the sound, the incense, the flowers, and the small shrine. One woman, a grey-haired, conservatively attired, South African senior citizen, stopped, stared, and demanded of the nun, "What are you doing?" Receiving no response, she turned to me and shouted, "What is she doing?" I replied, "She is praying for the release of children from detention." The woman looked back at the nun. Then, turning her attention again to me, she posed what struck me as an unexpected, impossible, but, on further reflection, a particularly revealing question: "Is she Colored or European?" "She's a Buddhist," I quickly answered. This stopped her. She glared at me for what seemed like a very long time, and then, as if in resignation, she concluded, "Well I guess you can have European Buddhists."
>
> —David Chidester[1]

AFTER THIS LIBERATING PROCESS OF CONFESSION, FORGIVENESS, REPENtance, reconciliation, and re-membering back into one society, the spirit of ubuntu is woven into the tapestry of this community's Constitution demonstrating egalitarian concepts of freedom and equality promoting a move to religious pluralism from Christian hegemony.

1. Chidester, "Christians, Buddhists, Muslims," 82.

In light of the intense negotiations between the Afrikaner National Party and the African National Congress, which gave birth to a South African democracy in 1994, and the conditions for this transition, which were characterized in many ways by Christian ideals, this final chapter will turn attention to the elitism and exclusivism of Christianity. As seen throughout this study, Christianity has been a dominant influence in the South African community both in its use to support oppression and believers on the other side trying to make sense of how this same faith can also be utilized to support oppression of the other. In this chapter I will review the current principles that govern church-state relationships and show that it is not a separation of church and state. South Africa seeks to uphold religious practices in conformity with the egalitarian foundations of its new Constitution. It is not a secular state, however, because religion is not perceived as taboo. As a point of comparison, I will examine, evaluate, and critique the American establishment and free exercise clauses against the 1996 South African Constitution as well as other African countries' constitutional provisions relating to religious freedom.

Religious Pluralism and Christian Hegemony

The Western Church in the 15th century viewed other religions such as Islam, Hinduism, and Buddhism, as enemies to Christ that must be destroyed. With the arrival of Muslims in South Africa slaves on the one hand and Christian settlers in the 17th century on the other, religious pluralism became more pronounced. In the 19th century, Indians brought Hinduism and the East European Jews added more facets to the religious scene. Religious pluralism has always been a feature and a social reality of South Africa and is even reinforced by the fact that Christianity itself is plural in its methodology, theology, liturgy, and practice.[2]

Even though South Africa was a pluralist country the apartheid government enforced separation, prevented inclusion, and suppressed necessary inter-religious, inter-faith pluralism in the society. If their policies were dedicated to maintain integrity of cultural, social, and religious difference, it is odd that they did not promote a theo-politics of religious pluralism. For David Chidester, a Religious Studies theorist,

2. Lubbe, "Religious Pluralism," 208–9.

the goal of cultural, social, and religious integrity was a lie, which is clearly exposed in the Dutch Reformed church's rigid theological exclusivism. Difference was not of value. Instead economic, political, and military domination of a majority by a minority was of greater interest. Chidester suggests that this exclusive political domination of the majority could be seen as a theological extension of the exclusivist Christian conviction that the vast majority of humanity will be condemned to Hell.[3]

It was Calvinist Christianity that first found its roots in South Africa and was protected by the occupying Dutch East Indian Company. Lutherans were given freedom to worship in 1780. It was not until 1804 when religious freedom was granted to all; though, Muslims were not allowed to practice their religion in public—offenders were punished by death. If Muslims showed any interest in converting to Christianity, they were of course welcome to join Christian churches. It was only in this potential of conversion to Christianity that Muslims got any respect, dignity, and true freedom to worship. The government, thus, had undue influence on the Church with regard to people of other faiths. Even after the supposed granting of religious freedom, people of other faiths were regarded as objects of mission work. White Christians had to come to grips with the otherness of people of other faiths, which by in large were people of other colors. With the exception of a small number of Jews, White Muslims, and White Buddhists, all members of religions other than Christians were regarded as "Black," including Coloreds and Indians. White Christians were faced with the challenge that the otherness was both of color and creed; it was political and religious.[4]

Hegemony in Public Education

The exclusion of the religious and political others was clearly seen in South Africa's public education system. Christian nationalism and Christian values were impressed upon all through Christian National Education. Chidester proposes that the underlying element, utilized through Christian National Education to maintain control and prevent religious pluralism, was hegemony. Religious symbols, which represent the political interests of one group, became tools of hegemonic

---

3. Chidester, "Christians," 81.
4. Lubbe, "Religious Pluralism," 209–10.

domination and determined the religio-political order. This hegemonic domination led to privileged access to shared legitimating sacred symbols. Other religio-political groups were forced to subservience, marginality, and exclusion. It does not welcome integration within a community, but instead it isolates. The hegemonic appropriation of Christian sacred symbols by Afrikaner nationalists established privileged claims to biblical symbols, sacred history, legitimacy, and thus, sacred authority to rule in South Africa.[5]

Two subjects were of importance in public schools: Religious Education and Biblical Studies. Kitshoff and van Wyks' teacher-training manual, *Method of Religious Education and Biblical Studies*, offers an explanation of the differences between these two subjects. Biblical Studies is described as a subject that "busies itself with the Bible . . . to facilitate Christian nurture."[6] It encourages respect for the text as authoritative word of God. It instructs one to revere, obey, and submit to biblical demands that fulfill cultural and religious destinies. While Religious Education appears as an introduction to the literature and histories of world religions in American and British public schools, this was not the case in South Africa. Religious Education meant instruction in the Christian religion based on the Bible. It was state policy—the Act for Education and Training (Act 90 of 1979)—that education should be Christian in character. While Jews, Muslims, Hindus, Buddhists, traditional African religions, and other religious groups were present in South African society, they disappeared in the Christian National Education, because Biblical Studies and Religious Education was all about the Bible, specifically a narrow view of the Bible.[7]

Kitshoff and van Wyk provide three reasons why Biblical Studies and Religious Education focused on the primarily Afrikaner interpretation of the Bible. The manual states, "this is a Christian country."[8] The 1984 Constitution affirms this in its opening. But what does the label "Christian country" mean? Does it automatically imply that the political order operates on Christian principles? Or, is it meant to prevent all possibilities of religious pluralism? The manual secondly asserts, "without

5. Chidester, "Religious," 6.

6. Kitschoff and Van Wyk, *Method of Religious Education*, 2. Quoted in Chidester, "Religious," 7.

7. Chidester, "Religious," 7.

8. As quoted in ibid., 8.

knowledge of the Bible the lives of people would be much the poorer."[9] Students in Black schools—the dispossessed—are forced to accept the very sacred symbol which gave legitimacy to their dispossession. They were told that the riches of the Bible are all they need to nourish the hunger felt with dispossession. Kitshoff and van Wyk provide a third reason for Biblical Studies and Religious Education provided by claiming "a child who follows the Christian faith is more likely to behave in a moral way than a non-Christian or an unreligious child."[10] A substantial explanation as to how this could be convincingly argued in the company of Jews, Muslims, Hindus, Buddhists, humanists, traditional Africans, and others in the country is not offered. Once again, Christian National Education (CNE) utilized Christian hegemony to prevent possibilities of an integrated society, which would demand conversations for religious pluralism.[11]

Chidester's hegemonic theory is indeed plausible, but one wonders whether the CNE's actions can be seen as purely a political tool to prevent religious pluralism. What influence did the profound religious convictions of the Afrikaner, which were deeply rooted in Dutch Calvinism, have on the education system? Theologian Irving Hexham draws from Brian Bunting's *The Rise of the South African Reich*, where Bunting refers to the "received opinion" on Christian National Education.[12] The cultural arm of the Broederbond, the Federation of Afrikaans Cultural Societies, reinstated the CNE in 1939 following the Second Anglo-Boer War. Its main purpose was to indoctrinate the young. He asserts that the term "Christian National Education" was a way to evoke an emotional response and to revive the memory of post-war resistance movements, affirming continuity with the Afrikaner past. Its desire was to resist British political domination and served the needs of the militant Nationalist. The received opinion claims that at a time when opposing British rule was difficult and impractical, the CNE was a means of expressing dissatisfaction and indirect political pressure to Britain.[13]

---

9. As quoted in ibid.
10. As quoted in ibid.
11. Ibid., 8.
12. See Bunting, *The Rise of the South African Reich*, passim.
13. Hexham, "Religious Conviction," 13–14.

While this may have satisfied the militant Nationalist by stirring indirect pressure on the British authorities without direct confrontation, there were other Calvinists and preachers who saw the CNE as more than the received opinion. S. J. du Toit (1847–1911) introduced the CNE in 1870. Jan Lion-Cachet (1838–1912) and leaders of the Reformed Church further developed it. Du Toit sought to apply the teachings of Calvinism into all areas of life, acknowledging a debt to Dutch Calvinism and the success of nineteenth century revival that produced a Christian school movement, trade unions, and a political party in the Netherlands. It was through the success and direction of Groen van Prinsterer (1801–1876), and Abraham Kuyper (1837–1920), that du Toit and other Calvinists introduced CNE to South Africa. Hexham contends that if the CNE in South Africa was a result of its development and practice in the Netherlands then the "received opinion" becomes untenable. It did not originate in South Africa following the Second Anglo-Boer War as the received opinion posits and it was not an extension of the pre-war educational system.[14]

The Reformed Church and fellow Afrikaners joined to establish the CNE system as a way to resist the Anglicization of Minister Lord Milner's policies. The Reformed Church and Afrikaner leaders played a key role in training school teachers in the theories of Christian Nationalism to further the cause of CNE. If the CNE was not a tool produced by the Afrikaner to further its political objectives, then for Hexham, it was an important element in the creation of the Nationalist ideology itself. It helped create the distinctive features of Nationalism. The effectiveness of the CNE as an ideological factor in the creation of Afrikaner nationalism can be seen in the way Reformed Church members identified with the Nationalist cause, which was deeply rooted in the church's understanding of Calvinism. Van Prinsterer, who had tremendous influence on Dutch Calvinists in the nineteenth century called his members to the source of their religion, namely the Bible. He challenged them to apply the source to all areas of their life. In his opinion, only a thorough Christian way of life could resist unbelief and revolution. He charged, "if Christian parents wanted their children to grow up as true Christians they could not entrust their education to deceptive liberal teachers who would undermine the power of the Gospel

---

14. Ibid., 14–15.

by their rationalism."[15] Therefore parents had to make sure that their children were educated in accordance with Calvinist truths. Parents' negligence of this serious obligation meant a betrayal of their baptismal promise to God in rearing their children in the knowledge and fear of God.[16]

Dutch Calvinists spent the latter half of the nineteenth century fighting the state on what became known as the "School Question." They took their Christian parental duty serious. They did not want to send their children to public schools and fought the state for subsidies for private schools. They claimed as taxpayers, they had the right to educate their children according to what made them feel safe and comfortable, not according to what the government prescribed. They wanted schools to be controlled by the parents of the children who attended them. In sending a child to school they argued parents delegated their God-given authority over the child to the schoolteacher. The liberals in Dutch politics resisted this narrow ideology, which led the Calvinists to form a united political front that gave rise to the first modern political party in the Netherlands under the leadership of Abraham Kuyper in 1879, the Anti-Revolutionary Party. Kuyper developed van Prinsterer's theories. Kuyper's charisma, creativity, ability to organize, and vision made him popular among his followers. They felt a sense of unity and a conviction that they would win. And, win they did. Thus, when Kuyper entered Dutch parliament in 1901, he passed the school legislation and changed the structure of Dutch education.[17]

The school question in the Netherlands was an important element in Dutch society because it focused on a whole range of developments and changed the character of the culture. The Calvinists now had control of their children's education. The freedom of their children's education was identified with their freedom of religion. Opposition was seen as an attack to their faith.

Likewise, in South Africa, the need for CNE became an accepted part of the Calvinist faith of the Reformed Church. The Nationalist Party was founded in 1914, in large part through the support of the Reformed Church. In response, the party made concessions to the convictions of

---

15. Ibid., 17.
16. Ibid., 16–17.
17. Ibid., 18.

the church. The Program of Principles published in 1914 shows the Party's support for CNE.[18] Reference is made to "the guidance of God," and the "people's life along Christian national lines." In the education section, reference is made to "the right of parents to choose the direction of their children's education." The "sphere of work" and "sovereignty in each sphere," derived from Kuyper's theory of "sphere sovereignty," justified this political stance. The Program of Principles was drawn and published by Willem Postma. It was revised by a committee, which included Postma and Professor Jan Kamp, who was on Kuyper's editorial staff of the daily newspaper *De Standaard* before emigrating to South Africa. One should not be surprised, then, about the Dutch Calvinist influence in the National Party's policy making.[19]

Hexham proposes that the main purpose of the CNE was to promote the interests of Calvinism. It was not intended as a device to indoctrinate the young in apartheid theory. He contends that one of the most valuable elements of the CNE both in the Netherlands and South Africa is that it incited Calvinists into political action. He proposes that while the CNE may have given legitimization to aspects of apartheid through its close ties and support of the National Party, it may have also contributed to the development of Afrikaner racial attitudes. However, the primary focus of the CNE, was the preservation of Calvinism, and only to the extent of this identifying with the Afrikaner has it been a factor in the development of apartheid. In other words for Hexham, CNE in South Africa was truly a religious conviction rooted deeply in Dutch Calvinism.[20]

Dispositions toward the Other

There is much validity to Hexham's proposals. The CNE was initially the product of a strong religious conviction. However, somewhere along the way, the proponents of the CNE, through their close ties with the policies of the National Party, lost sight of its initial purpose. As they got more involved in the politics of the National Party they gave legitimacy to the policies of apartheid and racial discrimination, and thus once

---

18. This publication is referred to frequently in ibid., from where the following information is taken.
19. Ibid., 19–20.
20. See especially ibid., 20.

again melded the theological and political. As one having been raised in this context and having experienced the educational system, I can attest to the role of the CNE in the validation of apartheid attitudes. What better system is there to instruct, control, and indoctrinate the youth of all races than the educational system? Children were taught from an early age that the White race is the superior race and most suited to rule and dominate? Whether or not on accepts Hexham's proposals, it seems clear that the Afrikaner became more comfortable with its exclusive separatist ideology and used the CNE as a strategy for hegemonic political domination. Therefore, I want to revisit Chidester's proposal of a religio-political imperative toward otherness. I want to show how the spirit of ubuntu is echoed in the embracing and inclusive principles of this proposal.

In Chidester's disposition toward otherness, he concludes that, "every us has a disposition toward them . . . what any us cannot do is ignore them. An intrinsic religio-political imperative requires every us to somehow come to terms with them."[21] "Us-ness" is contingent on our relationship with "them." Chidester proposes four orientations as a strategy in adopting a religio-political imperative, beginning with the most violent and concluding with the least violent disposition toward otherness.

He believes first that the strategy of *exclusion* is a violent method of elimination. "Us" becomes an exclusive, single group, where the group believes that its memebrs are the chosen ones, the chosen race, they belong to the one true church, and that there is only one biblical salvation and that unity in a world of religio-political multiplicity is dealt with violent methods of exclusion. This aversion to otherness is a violent strategy to eliminate all possibilities of pluralism.[22] Other faiths are seen as nothing but objects for Christian mission. With the divisive ideology of apartheid in 1948, Muslims, Buddhists, Hindus, and traditional African religionists were separated spiritually and physically. The only evidence of any vague form of religious pluralism was the Jewish presence in which otherness was more creed than color. Although, the largest group of Christians in South Africa is Black, political agendas were more important than religious kinship. Black Christians were

21. Chidester, "Religious," 12.
22. Ibid., 13.

excluded due to their color, although their faith was a product of White missionaries.[23]

Second, the strategy of *hegemony* is a less violent method toward otherness and is accomplished overtly. As seen in the public education of South Africa the violation of difference is achieved by the sacred symbols of one particular group. Religious plural beliefs of otherness, are explained with hegemonic terms by the ideology of the dominant group. Ancestors are replaced by demons; other religious beliefs become superstitions. Hegemony is established by giving validation to the dominant political interests with Christian religious symbols.[24] The preamble of the apartheid Constitution reads, "In humble submission to Almighty God who controls the destinies of peoples and nations ... to uphold Christian values and civilized norms, with the recognition and protection of freedom of faith and worship."[25] In 1985 hundreds of Muslims joined Blacks on the streets of Cape Town in protest against the totalitarian government. Several Muslims were detained and a year later the DRC warned against Muslim involvement in revolutionary action. In 1986 the DRC pronounced that Islam was a false religion and a threat to Christianity in South Africa and the world.[26]

The strategy of *toleration* toward otherness is a religio-political compromise, in which no one group is more powerful to establish any form of dominance over others. In the US, religious toleration embodied in the First Amendment is a negotiated compromise that guarantees religious freedom and liberty so that no one group can enforce its will and power over another. Therefore, in order to protect the rights and liberty of one it is necessary to ensure the freedom of all.[27]

In South Africa though tolerance is perceived, not intended, since the other religions consider themselves as being tolerated, but not free, therefore Lubbe contends that religion and racism is closely connected in theory. Every experience of race is also interpreted as an experience of religion. Members of other faiths contend that as long as they are not politically free, they are not religiously free. The perceived attitude

23. Lubbe, "Religious Conviction," 211.
24. Chidester, "Religious," 13.
25. Lubbe, "Religious Conviction," 211.
26. Ibid., 212.
27. Chidester, "Religious," 13.

of the State toward these members is that they are religiously tolerated, but not religiously free. Once again, the religious tolerance that existed during the apartheid era was in fact yet another mode of exclusion and avoidance of religious pluralism.[28]

These three strategies seem to represent different aspects of one over-arching strategy in the context of South Africa. "Hegemony . . . extended through . . . hegemonic explanations of otherness by which plural religious beliefs, practices, and experiences are forcibly re-explained in terms by the singular ideology of a dominant group."[29]

Apartheid's Revelation of Christianity

Presently three quarters of South Africa's population attest to some form of Christianity. Although Christians played and are playing a significant role in the post-apartheid era, the fact that those calling themselves Christians were involved in the creation of the apartheid regime makes it necessary to turn a critical eye toward the religion and ask about its credibility. Only in a constructive critique that demands liberation of Christianity, can it then fulfill its true potential as a force to humanize and provide greater justice to society. Any form of legalized and enforced discrimination based on the color of one's skin, which is shaped and supported by Christian principles, is a violent denial of the egalitarian and universal message of love of its founder Jesus. I wish to highlight the problems within the teachings of Christianity, in light of its support of apartheid and apartheid-era South Africa as a Christian country. In contrast, I offer examples of how Christians in the new democracy have helped in the healing of this broken country. Sincere and authentic healing cannot be achieved in any society unless truth of the past and present is exposed, faced, and dealt with, as shown in the Christian influence in the South African TRC. The success of the TRC there was due in large part to the strong positive influence of Christians in the country and on the TRC Commissions. In this discussion one sees Christian ideals used for bad (apartheid era) and good (post-apartheid era).

History and Philosophy of Religion scholar Martin Prozesky says that it is one thing to declare apartheid a heresy by condemning

28. Lubbe, "Religious Conviction," 212.
29. Chidester, "Religious," 13.

a morally offensive system, but that condemnation does not provide answers as to how an orthodox group with orthodox convictions can devise, implement, and support a system that is a major departure from orthodoxy. Condemning apartheid as heresy speaks to the effect but not to the cause. Prozesky believes further that without a sincere search for the cause, Christianity is prevented from being a positive influence in society. Because of its undesirable ethical stance and its loss of credibility, people of other faiths and religions are less apt to support Christianity.[30]

Prozesky's criteria for critiquing Christianity are formulated around the universal love of Jesus. He contends that White Christians must come to grips with the fact apartheid South Africa failed disgracefully and was incompatible with the basic elements of Jesus' universal love. The commitment to loving ones fellow beings as oneself involves equality, care, support, and wellbeing for all South Africans. Anything short of this cannot be real love and contradicts the central message of Christianity's founder. This is not a problem for White Christians in South Africa only. White Christians colonized the world, introduced slavery, and almost made the Native Americans extinct and possessed their land. They gave us the Holocaust and Hiroshima. The point here, however, is that this religion which claims to have salvation for all of humanity through Christ, has been associated with some of the world's worst atrocities and human rights violations. Not to forget too, this is the same religion that condemns those without salvation through Christ to hell.[31]

In the preface of Immanuel Kant's *Critique of Pure Reason*, he writes,

> Our age is, in a special degree, the age of criticism, and to criticism everything must submit. Religion through its sanctity, and law-giving through its majesty, may seek to exempt themselves from it. But they then awaken just suspicion, and cannot claim the sincere respect which reason accords only to that which has been able to sustain the test of free and open examination.[32]

---

30. Prozesky, *Christianity Amidst Apartheid*, 125.
31. Ibid., 128.
32. Kant, *Critique of Pure Reason*, 7.

Words written over two centuries ago very aptly describe what the Christian religion and the government in South Africa sought to do—exempt themselves from criticism. In the process they subjected themselves to suspicion and disrespect. Instead it divided and almost destroyed this society. Prozesky contends that "apartheid shows just how easily even devout believers in a heavily Christianized culture can unwittingly make their faith into an effective component of group self-interest in the forms of nationalist domination and economic exploitation."[33] When one reads the Bible at face value without the luxury of sophisticated tools for varying interpretations, it does not give a clear egalitarian treatment of humanity. Rather it focuses more on conquering and domination. What one concludes from biblical history is that survival depends on domination. If the Bible was clearer on egalitarian social teaching then opposition to slavery and other social inequalities would have taken place a lot sooner than it has. Instead, the Bible is loaded with models of domination that seem to further discourage an egalitarian message of universal love that embrace all. Israel suffered oppression from many nations. Before the Israelites were freed from slavery in Egypt the first-born Egyptian children were put to death in a divine act. This hardly constitutes a move toward universal egalitarian benevolence. This type of model, along with several of Israel's violent successes as the chosen nation, could lead some to understand violence as God's way of accomplishing things for God's people. Another group of people in another time who also felt chosen by God would have no reason to choose a non-violent, egalitarian approach to governance. If the Bible is the authoritative word of God, divinely inspired and written, then one cannot understand how its followers take these models seriously and apply it to their history.[34]

Prozesky makes another intriguing point regarding Christianity and its salvific emphases. He finds Christianity's traditional view of salvation a serious problem and a contradiction of Jesus' message of universal love for all.[35] Since Christianity claims to be the only religion blessed with the keys to eternal life, the Christian view of salvation itself can be deemed elitist and exclusivist, a contradiction to the spiritual

---

33. Prozesky, *Christianity amidst Apartheid*, 129.
34. Ibid., 130–31.
35. Ibid., 133.

model of embracing all. To say that God's gift of salvation to all human beings can be only received through Christianity is elitist. It's exclusivist to further admit that this free salvation is through Christ alone. A religion that claims that its way is the only true way to believe and non-acceptance of its faith will lead to damnation must be viewed with extreme suspicion and caution when these condemnatory ideas find there way into political actions. Christian pluralists reject this form of elitism and exclusion. We must reject this spiritual apartheid. If Jesus taught of unconditional and universal love, why is His salvation limited to just those who accept His teachings only?

In the discussion of minjung theology, I highlighted a strength of the people hermeneutic was its redemption of the prominence of the historical Jesus. It is much easier to identify with Jesus as a human person rather than a deified anthropomorphic personification. This can be viewed as a weakness or distortion to much Evangelical theology because it seems to take significance away from the resurrected Christ. People can identify with the historical Jesus of suffering and pain and his mission to alleviate the class, gender, and social barriers, which much consumed much of his earthly mission. Many Evangelicals, including a good portion of South Africa's White Christians, are consumed with the afterlife and their security of salvation in heaven through Christ. Therefore, the resurrected Christ is central to their worldview and spirituality. This can explain why some Christians like the Afrikaners, could sincerely support the injustice of apartheid with deep religious convictions.

Further, to say that Jesus Christ is the unique salvific mediator denies salvific roles of other religions like Buddhism, Hinduism, Islam, and Judaism. It is not difficult to see why these exclusivist and elitist teachings could lead to the Afrikaners discriminatory and non-egalitarian methods to control since they believed like Israel, they were the chosen. The egalitarian and universal concepts of Jesus' teachings did not fit well with the architects of apartheid, because they understood Christianity in non-egalitarian, elitists, and exclusive terms.[36]

---

36. Ibid., 132–34.

Constitutional Implications for Religious Pluralism

The political and legal system of pre-1994 South Africa was particularly noted for the totalitarian interference of the state in the private sphere of people's day-to-day lives. In apartheid South Africa, the state prescribed, with race as the prime criterion, whom one could marry, where one could reside and own property, which schools and universities one would be allowed to attend, and which jobs were reserved for persons of a particular race. The state dictated to sports clubs whom they could admit as members and against whom they were permitted to compete. The sick had to be conveyed in racially exclusive ambulances, could only receive blood transfusions from donors of their own race, and only qualified for treatment in racially defined hospitals. The state even regulated who would be allowed to attend church services in certain regions, and where one could be buried. These racist mandates of a totalitarian regime did not reflect the spirit of the victims they impacted, who constituted a vast majority of the South African nation. They also were not supported by the religious convictions of the people, or of a majority of the people, or for that matter of any distinct section of the people.[37]

The new South Africa has attempted to Africanize the country from the Western and European model which only benefited the White elite minority. It seeks to uphold African values in its institutions. In South Africa's totalitarian regime, however, two factors monopolized the country, namely 1) institutionalized discriminatory structures by the state, and 2) a bias to one religion, Christianity, and a particular view of Christianity at that. The power of the sword to enforce a dominant religion was a distinct feature of this regime. Although there was not an established state church, there were laws that gave the state a right to interfere in the affairs of religious institutions, to repress the total freedom and full practice of these religions under the Internal Security Act 21. If the Minister of Law and Order was of the opinion that an institution upheld communist influences it was subject to banning and had its privileges to worship denied. The history of apartheid was a repression of religious pluralism with an agenda, to preserve the national, ethnic, cultural, and religious identity of its own people.[38]

37. Van der Vyver, "Constitutional," 2.
38. Ibid., 1–3.

Therefore, the transitional Constitution of April 1994 was constructed under the rubric to eliminate such hegemony and provide social, political, and legal structures different from its past. In a way, it may have been designed as a reactionary response to its predecessors. It reads,

> While thus recognizing the injustices of our past… the new South Africa is an open and democratic society based on human dignity, equality and freedom . . . Any institution associated with the discrimination and repression of apartheid must be taken to be incompatible with the values embodied in the kind of society the country now aspires to be.[39]

South Africa's new Constitution was written with the intent to recognize from its tragic past and to avoid its repetition. Its history was one of repression, oligarchy, inequality, and secrecy. Its new Constitution set the foundation that made for a peaceful transition from oligarchy to democracy. After intense negotiations, a transitional Constitution was formulated in 1993. It was enforced on April 27, 1994, coinciding with the country's first democratic elections. This transitional Constitution served as a bridge of the repressive, unjust, and painful past, to a peaceful, democratic future, as the nation looked forward to a final Constitution. The 1993 transitional Constitution laid a solid foundation for the protection of rights in the final 1996 Constitution. The right to equality, freedom of expression, religious freedom, and freedom of association, were all part of this impressive catalogue of rights. Unlike the apartheid Constitution, religious rights were not subject to suspension during a state of emergency. The 1996 Constitution was set into action in February 1997. It was to impress upon all South Africans, tolerance.

There has been an escalation of conflicts along the lines of religious, ethnic, and civilization that have surfaced in recent history. A resurgence of nationalism is a considerable factor toward this increasing aggression internationally. Nationalism spun the two great world wars and the more recent conflicts in India, Pakistan, Palestine, Israel, Kosovo, Sri Lanka, Afghanistan, Iraq, Iran, and the United States. Nationalism promotes the idea that one particular nation is superior to other nations. The attitude of many Americans is a fine example of this. Tolerance encourages the idea that all are equal, that no nation, race, or

---

39. Ibid., 3–4.

religion is superior to another, while nationalism manipulates the feelings of inferiority through conversion to a superiority mentality.[40]

Affirmative tolerance, according to Lourens du Plessis means that people make a concerted effort to understand a desire to accept, and appreciate one another. Passive tolerance is people just putting up with one another.[41] Although, passive tolerance is more welcome than no tolerance at all, the 1996 Constitution aimed at a high level of affirmative tolerance. It made special provisions for particularities that arise out of a diversity of religious individuals and communities. Because reconciliation is a high priority to South Africa for nation building, the preamble of the final Constitution alludes to the significance reconciling and connotes positive or affirmative tolerance. The era of the Afrikaner Christian hegemony ended with the enforcement of the 1996 Constitution. The conciliatory preamble reads,

> We, the people of South Africa, Recognize the injustices of our past; Honor those who suffered for the freedom in our land; Respect those who have worked to build and develop our country; and Believe that South Africa belongs to all who live in it, united in our diversity.
>
> We therefore, through our freely elected representatives, adopt this Constitution as the supreme law of the Republic so as to: Heal the divisions of the past and establish a society based on democratic values, social justice and fundamental human rights; Lay the foundations for a democratic and open society in which government is based on the will of the people and every citizen is equally protected by law; Improve the quality of life of all citizens and free the potential of each person; Build a united and democratic South Africa able to take its rightful place as a sovereign state in the family of nations. May God protect our people.[42]

The 1983 Afrikaner Constitution proclaimed; "The people of the Republic of South Africa acknowledge the sovereignty and guidance of Almighty God." In the 1996 Constitution, the name of God is used only in the closing phrase of the preamble. God is called to protect. In the opening lines of the national anthem God is asked to bless Africa and is repeated in the six official languages of the country. Du Plessis

40. Smith, "Protecting," 6.
41. du Plessis, "Freedom," 2.
42. du Plessis, "Freedom," 3–4.

validly contends that the reference to God in the closing of the preamble seems to favor a monotheistic belief. While tolerance and reconciliation are high priorities for the new democracy, one wonder whether favoring monotheism could be viewed as intolerant toward polytheists and atheists.[43] Similarly, while the religious favoritism might well be against non-monotheists, some Christians could find the reference to God offensive in that it seeks to maintain neutrality in respect to all religions. One could contend this belittles the divine deity, which leans toward idolatry. But, maybe this is exactly what the Constitution attempts to achieve—religious practices in conformity with egalitarian foundations.

The change from Christian hegemony, which stifled religious pluralism, to religious freedom, demonstrates the importance of fundamental human rights in the Constitution and an embrace of ubuntu ideology, a true African spirituality. The drafting of the Final Constitution consisted of a Constitutional Assembly (CA), which was comprised of the National Assembly and the Senate. Four hundred and ninety representatives from seven political parties made the CA. Also, the public was involved in the negotiation process toward the Final Constitution. To make this a true democratic process, and in the spirit of ubuntu, the CA made a working draft available to the public in October 1995 with requests to receive submissions from the public about their Constitutional concerns. The CA decided to use language that was understandable by its citizens. They published a newsletter called Constitutional Talk. This newsletter informed the people about the progress of the constitutional process. People were invited to discussion groups to clarify misunderstandings. A useful internet homepage included CA minutes and reports, databases of submissions, issues of previous newsletters, media statements, and draft texts. A Talk-Line provided information by telephone. The public involvement with the Constitutional process proved to be successful in the constructing of the Final Draft.[44]

The Constitution endorses human rights over popular majority concerns. As an example, it is believed that over 80% of South Africans favor capital punishment, but the Constitution does not endorse the

---

43. Ibid., 4.
44. Blake, "Religious," 4.

death penalty. Almost the same percentage oppose abortion but again the Constitution provides for the right to one's choice. Since conservative Christianity has enjoyed a major in the country, it would be safe to say that a greater percentage reprehend the idea of homosexuality, but the Constitution protects discrimination based on sexual orientation.[45] The largest number of submissions from the public revolved around the guarantee of equality based on sexual orientation. Section 9 of the Constitution sees the Church as a juristic person. Although homosexuality may be a violation of a Church's doctrine, it will be in violation of human rights if membership is denied to a person of gay or lesbian orientation. A more controversial issue arose around the gender of clergy. Many churches still discriminate clerical roles based on gender. Women may not be allowed to enter the vocation or seek ordination in some denominations due to the denomination's beliefs and bylaws. A lively debate revolved around the Roman Catholic Church and their refusal to ordain women as priests and their discrimination against gays and lesbians. A strict reading of Section 9 would interpret the Roman Catholic Church's practice as illegal under the South African Constitution. The Church cannot discriminate on any ground unless they can prove that such discrimination is fair. The Church is then required to prove fairness in a court of law. The equality section in Section 9 may be construed at odds with the rights associated with freedom of religion. However, the designation of the Church as juristic person puts it under the prohibition that "no person (including juristic persons) may unfairly discriminate directly or indirectly on any ground."[46]

The union between the church and state during apartheid certainly provided legal preferences for the DRC. However, it is interesting to note that the 1996 Constitution does not make a separation between church and state. Given the historic past of the Afrikaner government, one would think that South Africans would call for a total separation of church and state. During the Constitutional drafting, controversy erupted around this very issue of separation. Archbishop Desmond Tutu called for a secular state. It should not come as a surprise that Tutu would call for a secular state, since the history of the previous Christian State was a tragic one. However, 3000 Christians marched to

---

45. Van der Vyver, "Constitutional," 6.
46. Blake," Religious," 4–5.

parliament to protest a proposal to separate church and state. Protesters included Christians ranging from Charismatic denominations to the DRC. Consequently, God was mentioned in the preamble, which makes South Africa and Zambia as the only coutnries in Southern Africa to discuss religious themes in prefatory language.[47]

Christo Lombaard provides two trends of policy on religion: a flat view of religions and a non-American type of separation of church and state, which Lombaard terms a "homegrown" separation of church and state.[48] The first trend suggests that all religions are equal, both legally and essentially. Only extremists will promote the idea that one religion should be given preference over others. If all religions are equal in the eyes of the state then philosophically the state sanctions that all religions provide ways to the same deity such as many Indian and Eastern Religions promote. This would be a comfortable trend for most governments to adopt especially if their citizens represent a broad variety of religious beliefs and practices. The flat view of religions would not be bogged down with issues of history, dogma, and liturgy. Rather, it would focus on similarities in an effort to promote dialogue and harmonious co-existence in the interest of democracy.

"Homegrown" separation of church and state is similar to the America's position, which in theory calls for a total separation of church and state. Lombaard posits that the American policy in practice echoes traits of fundamentalism and possible authoritarianism. Absolute church-state separation has to be adhered to the extent that all minutiae of public life have to be legislated. This just accentuates an extreme form of nationalism where prayers are replaced with patriotic singing of the national anthem and religious symbols are substituted with the display of the national flag. Due to the importance of religion to South African citizens it is incorporated rather than excluded and most visible in state functions. The state does not remove itself but gives religions equal space without religious preferences to one over the other.

Religious Rights and Freedom

Discriminatory state polices and religious persecutions resulting in atrocious human rights violations have occurred even in more secure

47. Ibid., 3–7.
48. For more on the following discussion see Lombaard, "The Left," 2–3.

countries. These policies are in violation of the freedom of thought, conscience, and religion principles of the 18th Article of the Universal Declaration. Almost six million Coptic Christians faced threats in Egypt, resulting in the attack of several Coptic businesses and churches and the deaths of eight people by extremists. Iran's government executed one Baha'i, detained fourteen others, including six awaiting the death penalty for the practice of their faith. Religious leaders and Christians, particularly those ascribing to the Greek Catholic Church were targets of bombings, violence, and the murder of a priest in Turkey. The Ahmadis in Pakistan are sentenced to life imprisonment, since the preaching of their faith is considered an attack and blasphemy to the Islamic religion. Buddhism enjoys preferential treatment and the practice is compulsory for all in the schools of Bhutan. Protestants, Catholics, Tibetans, Buddhists, and Muslims continue to face religious repression and official control from the Chinese government. Shiite teachings in Malaysia are considered a national security threat to Islam, which results in imprisonment. The Buddhist state in Myanmar practices discriminatory and intolerant policies toward Muslims and Christians by destroying mosques, schools, denying healthcare, civil service employment, education, and a revocation of citizenship. North Korea discourages religious activities unless it serves the interests of the state. Uzbekistan prohibits Christians to proselytize except in churches. Vietnam opposes unofficial religious activities.

In 1997, Russia adopted the limited citizen's religious freedom law imposing severe limitations on minority religious groups including some mainline Orthodox groups. A wait period of fifteen years is a requirement to obtain property, publish, operate schools, and conduct charitable activities. Many nations in Europe have set up enquiry commissions to investigate the spread of cults and sects with an increased attitude of xenophobia and hostility toward new religious movements. France identified 172 groups as sects in 1996, including Jehovah's Witnesses and the Church of Scientology. A report that identified these groups was formulated and publicized without the full knowledge of these minority groups. This contributed to an atmosphere of media libeling, circulation of false information and religious intolerance. Germany's commission investigated so-called sects and psycho-groups with an emphasis on the dangers of Scientology, but failed to recognize them as a religion.[49]

The death toll of the March 2002 Hindu Muslim riots in India reached over 1000 in one week. The riots were instigated by Hindu leaders who went on a rampage, looting, killing, raping Muslim victims, and destroying mosques, while the police stood by and watched. The Indian government by way of its inaction seemed to condone these acts of barbarism. Indian Muslims form part of India's economically depressed minority. The states apathy was seen in its failure to respond to these victims of hate.[50]

Section 15 of the South African Final Constitution categorically mandates the right to religious freedom: "Everyone has the right to freedom of conscience, religion, thought, belief and opinion."[51] It also makes room for those who choose to not believe in any religion at all.[52] The freedom of religion clause includes, "forbidding discrimination on the basis of religion, a clause discussing religious education, a provision dealing with oaths contrary to religious beliefs, and a freedom of association clause."[53]

Section 15 of the South African Constitution is conspicuously different than the clause on religion in the First Amendment in the American Constitution, which reads, "Congress shall make no law respecting an establishment of religion, or prohibit the free exercise thereof." The American statement is twofold. First, the establishment clause states that there shall be no official governmental action, which promulgates the establishment of a particular religion. Second, the free exercise clause declares the government shall not interfere with an individual's right to practice his or her religion as he or she sees fit. The religious influence during the colonization of America profoundly impacted the establishment of religious liberty in its Constitution.[54]

There is a difference of opinion on the language of Section 15 of the South African Constitution. Does it include establishment proscrip-

---

49. Smith, "Protecting the Weak," 7–9.
50. "Where is World Conscience," 1–2.
51. South African Constitution, Section 15, 1996, 1.
52. du Plessis, "Freedom," 6.
53. Blake, "Religious Freedom," 3.
54. Smith, "Protecting," 5.

tions as understood in the American Constitution, or is the protection of religious rights and freedom better of than the establishment clause? The establishment clause calls for a strict separation of church and state as well as a separation of politics and organized religion. Du Plessis informs that such a separation promotes freedom from religion rather than freedom of religion.[55] The establishment clause in the American Constitution serves to prevent advancing or inhibiting religion by the state, while the free exercise clause is to allow members of all religious backgrounds to pursue their faiths without any interference from the State. The essence of the notion of religious freedom is having the right to religious beliefs, to be able to declare beliefs openly without fear of intimidation. It also guarantees one the right to demonstrate one's beliefs in worship, practice, teaching, and that this freedom will be not stifled by forcing people to act in ways that will be contrary to their common beliefs and practices. Therefore, one could argue that Section 15 of the South African Constitution does not contain an establishment clause but rather focuses exclusively on free exercise. An example of the free exercise focus is found in the accessibility to radio and television given to religions. All religions with a substantial following are allowed to buy equal time to broadcast their religious services via the state controlled Radio and Television Corporation. Institutions are not permitted to buy extra airtime since it would defeat the egalitarian intent.

Although section 15(3) of the Constitution recognizes marriages under different religious, personal, or family systems, in an attempt to understand and support African values and African customary marriages, juridical actions thwart present and future marriages that are or will become polygamous.[56] It was traditionally held that Muslim marriages were polygamous and therefore should not be recognized legally whether the marriage was polygamous or not. The courts deduced that the very potential of a monogamous union could result in polygamy and concluded that it did not follow the mainstream jurisprudence. In a case regarding a divorced Muslim woman's claim for alimony, the Constitution, still prejudiced with its conventional language, maintained that the contract in a Muslim marriage violated good morals therefore any claim for alimony could not be enforced. This seems rather

---

55. du Plessis, "Freedom," 6.
56. Van der Vyver, "Constitutional Perspective," 17.

preferential and contradictory. While the courts attempt to understand and maintain African values and African customary marriages the verdict of the Muslim trial indicated that the Constitution recognizes but does not guarantee the rights of persons cultural, religious, and community practices. One can only conclude that this case questioned a public policy that tends to favor the preferences and prejudices of one group over the other.[57]

Religious Freedom Clauses in Southern Africa

Many countries in Southern Africa turned toward democracy in the 1990s. South West Africa became Namibia after South Africa ended its rule there. Multiparty elections took place in Zambia in 1991 after a history of one party rule. Malawi moved in the same direction in 1993. Free elections also took place in Lesotho. Five southern African countries improved freedom for its citizens and approved new constitutions. Many African constitutions include clauses promoting religious liberty, general freedom of religion, non-discrimination on the basis of religion, religious education, and oaths contrary to religious beliefs. Many African countries define the general freedom of religion right *via negativa*. The Zimbabwean Constitution is one such example:

> Except with his own consent or by way of parental discipline, no person shall be hindered in the enjoyment of his freedom of conscience, that is to say, freedom of thought and of religion, freedom to change his religion or belief, and freedom, whether alone or in community with others, and whether in public or in private, to manifest and propagate his religion or belief through worship, teaching, practice and observance.[58]

Other African countries define freedom of religion in a positive light as "everyone has the right to freedom of conscience, religion, thought, belief and opinion." The negative type is understood as no one's freedom of religion can be hindered, while the positive type reads as one has the right to freedom of religion. The latter grants freedom affirmatively and implies that hindrance of that freedom is strictly forbidden, while the former prohibits the hindrance of religious expression. Religious liberties of the negative type include the right to change,

57. du Plessis, "Freedom," 11.
58. Ibid., 5.

practice, and share religious beliefs. It also provides for one to consent to a derogation of one's religious rights and allows parents to limit their children's rights through discipline. While these limitations are absent in the positive type, the scope of religious liberties is by no means restrictive or narrow.

Most southern African constitutions prohibit discrimination on the basis of religion or creed. The distinction between religion and creed, however, is not always clear. Namibia, Lesotho, Malawi, and South Africa forbid discrimination based on religion, while other countries forbid it based on creed. No African court has defined creed, although Botswana's highest court argues that it is different from religion.[59] Webster's Dictionary defines creed as a, "formulation or system of religious faith." Five American courts and one Canadian court define creed in religious terms. It could be that Botswana, Swaziland, Zambia, and Zimbabwe, include political, social, and economic aspects to encompass a broader definition of creed. The absence of the word "religion" in their discrimination clauses does mean that discrimination based on religion is accepted.

There are two types of clauses, relating to religious education. One protects the right for an institution to establish their own schools and provide religious education. A second addresses compulsory religious education in public schools. Constitutions differ on the right to establish religious schools. Three countries grant the right to establish and maintain religious schools at their own expense; two countries do not grant this right, but do not prevent religious education to take place within that religious community. Three other constitutions allow "any person or everyone to establish private schools at their expense, providing that these schools maintain government educational standards."[60] No reference is made to compulsory religious education or observances in the Malawian and Namibian constitutions. South Africa and other countries promote freedom of choice, making attendance of religious ceremonies free and voluntary if it relates to a practice other than one's own belief.

Most African constitutions also allow for the protection from taking oaths, if it is contrary to one's religious belief. South Africa allows

---

59. See Blake, "Religious Freedom," 514–15.
60. Ibid., 535.

one to take an affirmation such as "so help me God," rather than an oath when being sworn into political office. Taking of an oath is not prohibited, but taking an oath that is contrary to one's own religious convictions could be seen as a violation of one's religious liberty and state coercion.[61]

Kenneth Kaunda, president of Namibia since 1964, was replaced by President Fredrick Chiluba in 1991 through the ratification of a new Constitution, which resulted in a multiparty democracy. After five years Chiluba amended the preamble of the Constitution to read, Zambia a "Christian nation but upholding the right of every person to enjoy that person's freedom of conscience of religion." This amendment was a constitutional breach and antithetical to the equality of peoples religious beliefs. Since then, there has been a number of recent incidents were Hindus have been the targets of hate crimes.[62] Christians have ostracized Hindus, which further encourages antagonism. Excluding the amendment in the prefatory language will help promote religious liberty in Zambia.

South Africa may be the strongest democracy in the area. Provisions have been made to protect the rights of persons to practice culture and religion. Though they are not perfect models for the rest of Africa and the world immediately to emulate, the direction is admirable and desirable. While Hindus and Muslims are still persecuted in many southern African countries by members of other religions, and countries are regressing on democratic commitments, South Africa seems to be leading the path for other southern African countries to follow.[63]

The American Establishment Experiment

America's commitment to religious freedom must be understood within the framework of its historical struggle for this very freedom. During the settlement in the 17th century, several colonies were established as sanctuaries for different sects and denominations. This plurality laid the foundation for religious freedom in the United States. Massachusetts and Connecticut were established by puritans seeking reform from the Church of England along Congregationalist lines. Although the New

---

61. du Plessis, "Freedom," 5–7.
62. Blake, "Religious Freedom," 538.
63. du Plessis, "Freedom," 2.

England Congregationalists and Puritans favored political freedom, they did not possess a good record when it came to religious tolerance. In fact, they resorted to similar forms of religious intolerance for which they fled from England. Roger Williams, Anne Hutchinson, and other non-conformists were expelled from the colony. Baptists were not allowed in the colony and four Quakers were hung when insisting on returning after being expelled. Roger Williams founded Rhode Island in 1630 on the principle of freedom of conscience and complete separation of church and state. Later other evangelicals and Baptists followed in the path of Williams's separation of church and state. Maryland and Pennsylvania soon incorporated the doctrine of free exercise of religion.[64]

Maryland was founded as a haven for Catholics from Protestant England in 1625 by George Calvert and his son Cecil. George Calvert was a convert to Catholicism. It was with Calvert's request from the new Protestant governor of Maryland to promise not to disturb Christians and Catholics specifically that the term "free exercise" first appeared in an American legal document in 1648. William Penn, a Quaker who was committed to finding a safe place for religious minorities, settled Pennsylvania in 1681. The great diversity of religions in Pennsylvania was indicative of its tolerance. In 1776, there were 403 different congregations in Pennsylvania. New York, New Jersey, and Pennsylvania became prominent Presbyterian colonies due to the influx of Scotch-Irish immigrants.

The rationalist ideas of the Enlightenment no doubt represented Thomas Jefferson's thoughts on free exercise. He wanted a wall between church and state so that there would not be a corrupting influence from either. Therefore, the establishment of freedom of conscience was fundamental to him in that it guaranteed to free the mind from outside bondage. At the end of the colonial era there were many different religious sects that existed, with no one sect large enough to establish a public state church. In the absence of this majority, the non-religious state provided the ideal situation for diversity and unity to take place among the colonies in the quest to protect religious liberty. James Madison who championed this sentiment at the constitutional convention said, "In a free government the security for religious rights consists

---

64. Smith, *Critique of Pure Reason*, 4.

in a multiplicity of sects." These practical considerations contributed to the strong separation of church and state, which guaranteed religious freedom in the United States Constitution.[65]

For Jefferson, the establishment of religious freedom, which prescribed religious liberty for all, was a fair and novel experiment. Christianity and all its forms must learn to stand on its own feet he said, "and on equal footing with the faiths of the Jew and the Gentile, the Mahometan, the Hindoo, and the Infidel of every denomination."[66] This proposal was very different from other western models, which proscribed that Christianity, as an established community must be protected from all other religions by the state. Jefferson wanted the growth of a religion to survive by its power to compel and convince, rather than by coercion of the state, and support by law.[67]

John Adams political experiment on religious liberty was engineered through the 1780 Constitution of Massachusetts. Like Jefferson, he wrote with equal inspiration that "authority in magistrates and obedience of citizens can be grounded on reason, morality, and the Christian religion without succumbing to other forms of ecclesiastical or civil tyranny."[68] While the Constitution guaranteed equal liberty and security of property for all people of all religions, it instituted a mild establishment of religion with special protection, preference, and privilege for types of Christian piety, morality, and charity. Both Jefferson and Adams were consciously involved in a new religious liberty experiment. The American Declaration of Independence, which they both drew, articulated the framework of their values: all are created equal with certain unalienable rights and every religion should be constitutionally recognized, protected, and possess essential rights and liberties.[69]

Jefferson's model of religious liberty involved two factors, disestablishment and free exercise of all religions. The state was not to show special preference or privilege to any one religion, nor should they make or affirm laws or policies on explicit religious grounds. The state should not depend on religious institutions to perform or carry out their

---

65. Ibid., 4–5.
66. Jefferson, *The Complete Jefferson*, 1147.
67. Witte, "A Most," 1.
68. Ibid.
69. Ibid., 1–2.

functions and should refrain from getting involved with the doctrines and disciplines of these institutions. The state should respect freedom of conscience and free exercise of all its subjects as inalienable and the most sacred of all human rights. Jefferson's experiment on religious liberty did not only influence Virginia but the entire nation.[70] Jefferson wrote:

> All attempts to influence it by temporal punishments, or burthens, or by civil incapacitations, tend only to beget habits of hypocrisy and meanness, and are a departure from the plan of the holy author of our religion . . . no man shall be compelled to frequent or support any religious worship, place, or ministry whatsoever, nor shall be enforced, restrained, molested, or burthened in his body or goods, nor shall otherwise suffer, on account of his religious opinions or belief, but that all men shall be free to profess, and by argument to maintain, their opinion in matters of religion, and that the same shall in no wise diminish, enlarge, or affect their civil capacities.[71]

Adams's model of religious liberty involved establishment of one public religion and the freedom of many private religions. He believed that every state needed to establish some form of public religion by law. Adams saw Jefferson's model as a philosophical fiction because he felt it was impossible to imagine that a state can successfully remain neutral and removed from religion. Yet, at the same time he was cognizant that it would be philosophical fiction for a state to coerce successfully all people to one common public religion. Therefore, he proposed that people should be able to make their own private decisions regarding matters of faith, for he regarded the rights of conscience to be indisputable, unalienable, indefeasible, and divine. He envisioned the creed of this public religion to be as follows:

> . . . honesty, diligence, devotion, obedience, virtue, and love of God, neighbor, and self. Its icons were the Bible, the bells of liberty, the memorials of patriots, the Constitution. Its clergy were public-spirited ministers and religiously-devout politicians. Its liturgy was the public proclamation of oaths, prayers, songs, and election and Thanksgiving Day sermons. Its policy was state

---

70. Jefferson, *Thomas Jefferson*, 957.
71. Gaustad, *Sworn on the Altar*, 13.

sanctions against blasphemy, sacrilege, and iconoclasm, state sponsorship of religious societies, schools and charities.[72]

Religious pluralism was essential in the maintenance and protection of religious and other forms of liberty. When asked about his personal religious affiliation, Adams responded, "Ask me not . . . whether I am a Catholic or Protestant, Calvinist or Arminian. As far as they are Christians, I wish to be a fellow-disciple with them all."[73] As a fierce patriot and a vigorous moralist, he knew that some would insist on establishment and others on freedom; therefore, he sought to appease both interests by proposing a tempered religious freedom with a slender religious establishment. He was convinced that the establishment of one common religion alongside other plural private religions' was fundamental for the survival of society and the state. "We must certainly begin," Adams wrote,

> . . . by setting our conscience free. For when all men of all religions consistent with morals and property, shall enjoy equal liberty . . . and security of property, and an equal chance for honors and power . . . we may expect that improvements will be made in the human character, and the state of society. But we must just as certainly begin by setting religion at the fore and floor of society and government . . . without religion, this world would be something not fit to be mentioned in polite, I mean hell."[74]

Conclusion

In this chapter, I highlighted the elitism and exclusivism of Christianity in the Christian National Education of the Afrikaner. The CNE was used to educate, propagate, and influence young South African children to grow up with the same ideologies of their parents and maintain an exclusive race, Afrikanerdom. I examined and evaluated the American establishment and free exercise clause in comparison with the 1996 South African Constitution and showed that even though religion played an integral part in South Africa's oppressive past in supporting oppression, she did not call for a separation of church and state but rather embraced

---

72. Witte, "A Most," 219.
73. Ibid., 233.
74. Ibid., 9–10.

religious pluralism in its Constitution to promote egalitarian values for all of its communities in true ubuntu spirituality.

America and South Africa lament a similar past and often their histories will instruct how to illuminate and modify current laws and Constitutions to overcome oppressive pasts rather than repeat them. In response to colonialism, the American Constitution forges a preferential status to the First Amendment freedoms and accordingly instilled essentially libertarian values in the fabric of all constitutional arrangements. South Africa's past is one of institutional discrimination. Therefore, human dignity and equal protection was a priority for the construction of a new Constitution. While the sentiments of libertarianism can be found in America's separation of church and state, South Africa strives for egalitarianism with hopes to provide a lucent model for its neighboring countries to follow. Religion is not treated as a government taboo for religious institutions to work out the details of its place in society, but rather the Constitution calls for an evenhanded treatment in official dealings.[75]

John Adams's 1780 Constitution strove for a balance between establishment of one public religion, namely Christianity, and the freedom of all private religions. Jefferson's model at the core was one of separation and religious individualism. Jefferson's model became the American model: separation of church and state. Adams proposed a more inclusive and embracing model, which at the heart aimed at accommodation and religious communitarianism. Whenever a state mandates by civil authority a public religion such as the Christian worship of God, it presumably hopes to promote happiness, order, and preservation of the state authority. However, invariably it promotes impiety, hypocrisy, and other oppressive evils. South Africa's past is one such example.[76]

Jefferson's model of separation and religious individualism would not have worked in the South African theme of ubuntu because it would have enforced a more rugged separation that already existed through apartheid. Separation compounded with isolation would result in the form of individualism that can be found in many Americans' extreme nationalism and patriotic arrogance. Adams' model of establishment of one public religion and the freedom of many private religions would

---

75. Van der Vyver, "Constitutional Perspective," 16–17.
76. Witte, "A Most," 213.

not work in South Africa either. Christianity was the established public religion under apartheid. Which other religion would be the new public established religion in the new democracy? Which religion would be effective as the established religion following the tragic legacy of Christianity? Accommodation and community, which are elements of Adams model, are essential elements to the new democracy, but religious equality was also fundamental to this new democracy. Therefore South Africa is neither a model of separation of church and state nor a secular state, but an egalitarian religious state promoting diversity, inclusivity, and community.

This chapter has shown that Christianity has been a dominant influence in South Africa although it is a religiously plural country. The Afrikaner used Christianity to separate, exclude, and suppress pluralism. The exclusion of otherness and other religious voices was clearly visible through Christian National Education, which was used as a political tool to procure hegemonic domination. I have shown why religious pluralists were and would be suspicious of the traditional elitist salvific view that many South African Calvinisits and Evangelicals hold. The exclusivist and elitist teachings lead to the Afrikaners' discriminatory and non-egalitarian methods to control because they believed, like the Israelites, that they were the chosen race.

South Africa's new Constitution drew lessons from its unjust and painful past. The right to equality, freedom of expression, religious freedom, and freedom of association were prioritized in the new Constitution. It was to promote affirmative tolerance with a celebration of religious pluralism, inclusivity, diversity, and community for healing, nation building, and national reconciliation. Ubuntu weaved its presence into the fabric of this once demoralized and segregated society. Now, in the present South Africa, a spirit that embraces all of humanity as persons interrelated in one common society pervades. Therefore, South Africa does not promote a separation of church and state, because she fervently seeks to uphold religious practices in conformity with the egalitarian foundations of her new Constitution. South Africa is not a secular state either, because ubuntu is necessary for this community's survival, growth, and maturity. Once a broken nation, South Africa is now on her way toward healing, reconciliation, repentance, forgiveness, and an embrace of democracy with egalitarian values. Ubuntu is the cement that holds this community together.

Conclusion

A Narrative Analysis of a Journey of Faith

South Africa today is viewed as a prime example of how a society can move beyond the bondage of racial factionalism to an egalitarian posture. In this society, the church has always played and will continue to play a prominent role. The church was influential in the transition to democracy and the political work to establish a just society. I contend that the church provided important ingredients for this peaceful transition. The Christian influence permeated South Africa's Truth and Reconciliation Commission and contributed to its success. Christo Lombaard emphasizes the religious influence of the TRC:

> One of the key features which has made the internationally admired South African Truth and Reconciliation Commission extremely difficult to emulate in other parts of the world, is the fact that someone with the religious gravity, moral integrity and political legitimacy of Desmond Tutu is not necessarily available to them.[1]

Hans Kung speaks about dialogability and steadfastness as two virtues. Dialogability for Kung is a deep democratic virtue, "which can only survive under the umbrella of a positive intellectual, cultural, and religious pluralism, under the reign of liberty, equality, and fraternity."[2] The apartheid government given its propensity to monopolize the truth adamantly did not see the need for dialogue. Kung describes the role of dialogability:

> Any regime, be it ecclesiastical or political, which is based on the absolute power of an individual or an oligarchy, a party or hierarchy, any regime that monopolizes truth with the help of juridicism, centralism, or triumphalism is essentially incapable

---

1. Lombaard, "The Left Governing Hand," 19.
2. Kung, "Dialogability," 237–38.

of dialogue. The tactics of survival may necessitate dialogue for a while, but it will never reach the roots of self-understanding; if it did, these systems of power would collapse like a house of cards. Therefore, dialogability is intrinsically a virtue critical of power and dominion ... Despots and potentates cannot tolerate their opposites as partners, only as subjects. Dialogue for them is equivalent to weakness; willingness to communicate means self-degradation. The price of such a relationship, which is built on command and obedience, is speechlessness. Those leading a dialogue do not want to impose their will on others; they do not perceive others any longer as a threat, but as an enrichment to life, not as competitors but rather as partners.[33]

The Black church cried for dialogue and understanding. Blacks wanted to be partners in an egalitarian and communitarian society characterized by ubuntu. They wanted to embrace difference, otherness, and celebrate diversity in an inclusive society. The Black church was steadfast in its attempt to keep the ubuntu hope alive that one day God may listen to its cries and respond. God's answer came 46 years later in ways that were previously unimaginable: democracy and the country's first Black president. This nation suffered terribly from oppressive rulers. The TRC did not repress the suffering from this nation's memory but rather to maintain dialogability it allowed the nation to confront the truth.

In Chapter 1, I showed how the Afrikaner government used Christianity to suppress the voice of the oppressed. The apartheid ideology discriminated and deprived Black people of fundamental human rights. The government lied, abused, killed, and had no tolerance for pluralism and diversity. In Chapter 2, I described how this government justified their policies with supposedly biblical concepts. Romans 13 was interpreted to call all citizens to be subject to their rule because they were ordained to lead this country. My alternative reading of the text concludes that Paul was addressing a chasm between the Roman Christians and the Jewish Christians. He wrote to the congregation asking them to be subject to the church governing leadership, for they are ordained by God to lead. This is not an unprecedented mandate to state authority giving them free reign to support abusive polices that suppresses freedom. The church must be the true light to the nations and question any regime, organization, or institution whether it be

3. Kung, "Dialogability," 239.

ecclesiastical or political, and operates on the premise of absolute power of an individual or an oligarchy. The church must be the moral voice to any institution that monopolizes truth for the interest and benefit of that particular institution.

In Chapter 3, I surveyed dominant hermeneutical trajectories in Latin America, Asia, and Africa. This study explored the model of a conversation with the text and showed how context is crucial in the fusion of two horizons, the text and context. Minjung theology retrieves the importance of the historical Jesus and His life here on earth since in our fixation of His resurrection we have almost forgotten that He was also human.

The influence of Latin American liberation theology and its hermeneutical trajectories has been emulated in contexts all over the world. Drawing from these trajectories South African Black theology continued to ask the difficult questions that western theological models hinder. Latin American liberation theology, Black theology, and feminist theology all claim that the experience of the oppressed is a privileged hermeneutical ground and that identification with the oppressed must always be the first act in understanding the Bible or our world today.

Although a narrative distinctiveness has permeated the whole project, it was made most explicit in Chapter 4: truth and reconciliation. I juxtaposed two governments: the National Party and the African National Congress. The former was nominally Christian and the latter exhibited Marxist influence. Forgiveness, truth, repentance, and reconciliation—fundamental New Testament Christian principles—were hallmarks of the TRC. Through them the TRC set a course that would achieve national healing through reconciling victims with perpetrators. The success of the TRC in comparison to similar commissions elsewhere was due to the strong Christian influence. This was a positive aspect of Christianity. Given its tragic past and in some ironic fashion, Christianity seemed to redeem itself through the process of the redemption of a people and a nation. Christians must constantly renew their convictions to radically commit themselves to speak out to the issues of human need for justice and equality for all. They must be the moral voice for the world. They cannot be half slave and half free. They must be the model for extremely radical ideas of love, truth, and goodness.

Chapter 5 focused on the value of difference in true ubuntu spirit. Apartheid excluded otherness. The use of Christian National Education maintained a hegemonic domination. Alternative religious voices were suppressed. I have shown how South Africa attempts to Africanize this country by moving away from a model of elitism and exclusion and now seeks to uphold ubuntu values of community and inclusion. Through provisions for freedom, and religious diversity, the new Constitution embraces otherness and celebrates community. It also provides a model for other countries in transition. Long before this miracle and transition to democracy South Africans dreamed that it could and can become a light to the nations.

Afterword

THE INTENT OF THIS AFTERWORD IS TWOFOLD. FIRST, I WANT TO PROvide an assessment of the current status of South Africa twelve years after democracy and provide reflections on what the ANC has done since coming to power in 1994. Second, I want to explore briefly what is the role of the church in light of this new democracy. I visited South Africa in January and September of 2004 and again in September and December of 2005 where I met with several leaders of church organizations. The following reflections are based on those conversations.

The country has moved from apartheid to a non-racial democracy, from antagonism with its neighboring states to common security and regional alliances. It has moved from a police state to police service, from capitalism and neo-colonialism to an African renaissance, from the Afrikaner as a "chosen" people to a moral renewal of the nation, from a narrow religiosity of Calvinism to a multi-religious nation. It has moved from an exclusionary separate development to a place that struggles to enforce ubuntu principles. The Constitution and its various commissions on human rights, gender, and youth have been significant and important for people to know that they have a Constitution that protects them with certain fundamental rights. In the first five years of the new democracy 3 million people gained access to clean water, 2 million households were connected to electricity and over 5 million children received health care and primary school nutrition. These programs continue to expand. When one looks at the challenges of the last 10 years and the progress made, the ANC has managed to strike a balance between cosmetic, short-term interventions and some long-term infrastructural changes. Housing, water, electricity, and road building in the previously disadvantaged communities, has certainly been a major and helpful intervention.

The gap between the rich and poor is still appalling and the unemployment and crime rate is higher than it was during the apartheid era. The ANC's job creation program is rather slow yet the economy is gradually growing. There is a clear understanding of how community structures work but unfortunately corruption at high levels of government has again disqualified some officials who are seen to be biased in their implementation of authority. The Inkatha Freedom Party and the ANC conflict at the regional level in Kwa Zulu Natal (KZN) province has been a decided impediment to progress. It would have been extremely helpful if the ANC had won KZN outright in the most recent elections, but they did not.

South Africans have shown an incredible capacity for reconciliation notably demonstrated in Mandela's lack of bitterness and in the TRC hearings. Co-existence and diversity are alive in the new South Africa. The ANC kept its non-racial vision, despite brutal repression. There is great religious and cultural tolerance, including recognizing the cultural rights of the Afrikaner. Expertise in negotiation has developed at all levels as people shape the new integrated government, which is resulting in a culture of ubuntu.

The role of the church during the transition from apartheid to democracy has varied. Before democracy the church was active and vocal, at least at a leadership level, but this did not represent all denominations. It was mostly the Catholic and Episcopalian churches that always were on the forefront of the struggle. The church was active and provided a space for political activity which political movements could not provide under its banned status. The church provided sanctuary for people involved in the struggle and gave a platform for planning and organizing the mass democratic movement and the protests of the late 1980's. Many church activists were involved at different levels of the struggle, from protest, to underground activity leading up to the elections. The church was very involved in voter registration and in democratic education, and could reach places in rural areas which would have been difficult for political organizations to reach.

However, the church seems to have lost its voice and is confused as to what its present role should be. During the apartheid years there was tremendous support from interfaith and ecumenical groups working together. It seems that the church expected this new government to bring change to the country almost immediately and did not forecast that its involvement in challenging the government and political developments should continue. Some churches were relieved that they could go back to being the church again, as if during the apartheid years the church had been forced into a different role, other than what it should be, a moral voice seeking justice and equality. Some people think that the church was somewhat burnt out and needed to re-group.

The church needs to raise its voice again and be the light it should be to the nation. It needs to be more proactive on the issues of crime and violence since South Africa has the highest crime, poverty, and HIV positive rates in the world, all of which stem from Black disillusionment with the ANC government for not producing changes to their lives and living conditions quickly enough. The church needs to fill the divide with programs in partnering with other non-governmental organizations and play a more prominent role than it does with the issues of HIV and the AIDS pandemic. It ought to rekindle its ecumenical and interfaith network in order to pool resources to tackle the huge social problems in South Africa. The HIV/AIDS problem and the current president's ruling out of ARV's has been a real slight on the people's ability to feel supported and cared for by the ANC. This isolates the poor, increases the distance between the people and government and reduces hope for those who really need it. Somehow it seems that churches are doing their own individual thing, rather than working together to provide more resources than any one group can. The ANC continues to ignore the AIDS pandemic and the impact this will have on the people and its economy. The church has the potential and moral fiber to make a valuable contribution and must unite to speak and act as one voice, challenging the ANC on the issues of health, welfare, and poverty as it did so successfully during the apartheid era.

Bibliography

Abineno, J. L. C. "The State, According to Romans Thirteen." *SEAJT* 14 (1972) 23.
Ahn, Byung-Mu. "Jesus and the Minjung in the Gospel of Mark." In *Voices from the Margin: Interpreting the Bible in the Third World*, new ed., edited by R. S. Sugirtharajah, 85–104. New York: Orbis, 1995.
———. "Jesus and People (Minjung)." In *Asian Faces of Jesus*, edited by R. S. Sugirtharajah, Faith and Culture Series, 163–72. New York: Orbis, 1993.
Alberts, Louw, and Frank Chikane, editors. *The Road to Rustenburg: The Church Looking Forward to a New South Africa*. Cape Town: Struik, 1991.
Amnesty International. "Argentina: Investigation into 'disappearances'—A Step towards Settling Outstanding Debt from 'Dirty War.'" June 11, 1998. No pages. Accessed July 23, 2007. Online: http://www.amnesty.org/en/library/asset/AMR13/010/1998/en/dom-AMR130101998en.html.
Apostolic Faith Mission Church. Pamphlet. *88 Years of Grace*. Johannesburg, 1996.
Asmal, Kader, et al. *Reconciliation Through Truth: A Reckoning of Apartheid's Criminal Governance*. New York: St Martin's, 1997.
Assmann, Hugo. *Theology for a Nomad Church*. Translated by Paul Burns. Maryknoll, NY: Orbis, 1975.
Bailey, Jackson, and Evangelina Hovino. "Developing Multicultural Organization." *JRBS* (1988) 14.
Baldwin, Lewis V. *Toward the Beloved Community: Martin Luther King Jr. and South Africa*. Cleveland: Pilgrim, 1995.
Bammel, Ernst and C.F.D. Moule. *Jesus and the Politics of His Day*. Cambridge: Cambridge University Press, 1992.
Barndt, Joseph. *Dismantling Racism: The Continuing Challenge to White America*. Minneapolis: Augsburg, 1991.
Barrett, C. K. *A Commentary on the Epistle to the Romans*. New York: Harper & Row, 1957.
Benson, Mary. *Nelson Mandela: The Man and the Movement*. New York: Norton, 1986.
Biko, Steve. *I Write What I Like*. London: Heinemann, 1978.
Blake, Richard Cameron. "Religious Freedom in Southern Africa: The Developing Jurisprudence." *BYULR* 2 (1998) 515–62.
Boesak, Villa. *God's Wrathful Children: Political Oppression & Christian Ethics*. Grand Rapids: Eerdmans, 1995.
Boff, Leonardo and Clodovis Boff. *Introducing Liberation Theology*. New York: Orbis, 1987.
Borg, Marcus. "A New Context for Romans XIII." *NTS* 19 (1972) 205–18.
Botha, Jan. *Subject to Whose Authority: Multiple Readings of Romans 13*. Atlanta: Scholars, 1994.

Boyer, Susan. "Exegesis of Romans 13:1–7." *Brethren Life and Thought* 32 (1987) 208–16.

Brown, Robert McAfee. "Diversity and Inclusiveness." *Church and Society* 67 (1977) 52–53.

Browning, Don S. *A Fundamental Practical Theology: Descriptive and Strategic Proposals*, Minneapolis: Augsburg Fortress Press, 1991.

Bunting, Brian Percy. *The Rise of the South African Reich*. Baltimore: Penguin, 1964.

Calvin, John. *Institutes of the Christian Religion*. The Library of Christian Classics 20–21. Translated by Ford Lewis Battles. Edited by John T. McNeill. Philadelphia: Westminster, 1960.

Cameron-Dow, John, editor. *The Miracle of a Freed Nation: South Africa 1990–1994*. Cape Town: D. Nelson, 1994.

Cheddo, Piero. *The Cross and the Bo-tree: Catholics and Buddhists in Vietnam*. New York: Sheed and Ward, 1970.

Center for Justice and Accountability. Accessed 2001. Online: http://www.cja.org/Romero.htm.

Chidester, David. "Christians, Buddhists, Muslims, and Others." *JTSA* 60 (1987) 81–86.

———. "Religious Studies as Political Practice." *JTSA* 58 (1987) 4–17.

Chikane, Frank. *No Life of My Own*. New York: Orbis, 1989.

Cleary, Edward. *Crisis and Change: The Church in Latin America Today*. New York: Orbis, 1985.

Concerned Evangelicals. *Evangelical Witness in South Africa: A Critique of Evangelical Theology and Practice by South African Evangelicals*. Grand Rapids, MI: Eerdmans, 1986.

Constitution of the Republic of South Africa, The. 1996.

Cullman, Oscar. *The State in the New Testament*. New York: Scribner, 1956.

Di Noia, J. A. "Jesus and the World Religions." *First Things* 54 (1995) 24–28.

De Gruchy, John W. *The Church Struggle in South Africa*. Grand Rapid: Eerdmans, 1986.

———, and Charles Villa-Vicencio. *Apartheid is a Heresy*. Grand Rapids: Eerdmans, 1983.

———. *Resistance and Hope: South African Essays in Honor of Beyers Naude*. Grand Rapids: Eerdmans, 1985.

Dowdall, Terry. "Theological and Psychological Reflections on Truth and Reconciliation Commission." In *To Remember and to Heal*, edited by Russel Botman and Robin Petersen. Cape Town: Human & Rousseau, 1996.

du Plessis, Lourens. "Freedom of or Freedom from Religion? An Overview of Issues Pertinent to the Constitutional Protection of Religious Rights and Freedom in the New South Africa." *BYULR* 2 (2001) 439–66.

Dunn, James D. G. *Romans 9–16*. WBC 38b. Dallas: Word, 1988.

Dussel, Enrique D. "Theology of Liberation and Marxism." In *Mysterium Liberationis: Fundamental Concepts of Liberation Theology*, edited by Ignacio Ellacuría and Jon Sobrino, 85–102. New York: Orbis, 1993.

Dyck, Harold J. "The Christian and the Authorities in Romans 13:1–7." *Direction* 14 (1985) 44–56.

Elliott, Neil. *Liberating Paul: The Justice of God and the Politics of the Apostle*. New York: Orbis, 1994.
Elphick, Richard. *Kraal and Castle: Khoikhoi and the Founding of White South Africa*. New Haven: Yale University Press, 1977.
Elphick, Richard and Hermann Giliomee, editors. *The Shaping of South African Society 1652–1820*. Cape Town: Longman Penguin, 1979.
Fowl, Stephen E. and Gregory L. Jones. *Reading in Communion: Scripture and Ethics in Christian Life*. Grand Rapids: Eerdmans, 1991.
Fredrickson, George M. *White Supremacy: A Comparative Study in American and South African History*. New York: Oxford University Press, 1982.
Friedman, M. *I Will Still Be Moved: Reports from South Africa*. Cape Town: Barker, 1963.
Gastrow, Shelagh, editor. *Who's Who in South African Politics*. 3rd ed. New York: Hans Zell, 1990.
Gaustad, Edwin S. *Sworn on the Altar of God: A Religious Biography of Thomas Jefferson*. Grand Rapids: Eerdmans, 1996.
Goodman, David. "Why Killers Should Go Free: Lessons from South Africa." *The Washington Quarterly* (1999) 169–81.
Gorgulho, Gilberto da Silva. "Biblical Hermeneutics." In *Mysterium Liberationis: Fundamental Concepts of Liberation Theology*, edited by Ignacio Ellacuría and Jon Sobrino, 123–149. New York: Orbis, 1993.
Grant, Robert M. and David Tracy. *A Short History of the Interpretation of the Bible*. 2nd ed. Philadelphia: Fortress Press, 1984.
Gutiérrez, Gustavo. *A Theology of Liberation: History, Politics, and Salvation*. Revised Edition. New York: Orbis, 1988.
———. "Statement by Gustavo Gutiérrez." In *Theology in the Americas*, edited by Sergio Torres and John Eagleson, 310. Maryknoll: Orbis, 1976.
Herzog, William R. "Dissembling, a Weapon of the Weak: The Case of Christ and Caesar in Mark 12:13–17 and Romans 13:1–7." *PRSt* 21 (1994) 339–60.
Hexham, Irving. "Religious Conviction or Political Tool?" *JTSA* 26 (1979) 13–21.
Hewson, Leslie A., editor. *Cottesloe Consultation: The Report of the Consultation*. Johannesburg, 1961.
Hollyday, Joyce. "Hearts of Stone." *Sojourners* 27 (1998) 44.
Horwitz, Robert B. "Truth Commissions, Nation-Building, and International Human Rights: The South African Experience and Reflections on the Politics of Human Rights Post 9/11." Accessed 2001. Online: http://communication.ucsd.edu/people/f_horwitz.html.
Hutchinson, S. "The Political Implications of Romans 13:1–7." *Biblical Theology* 21 (1971) 49–59.
Huttenback, Robert A. *Ghandi in South Africa: British Imperialism and the Indian Question, 1860–1914*. London: Cornell University Press, 1971.
Jefferson, Thomas. *The Complete Jefferson, Containing His Major Writings*, edited by Saul Kussiel Padover. Freeport, NY: Books for Libraries, 1943.
Johnston, Douglas. "Churches and Apartheid in South Africa." In *Religion, The Missing Dimension of Statecraft*, edited by Douglas Johnston and Cynthia Sampson. 177–207. New York: Oxford University Press, 1994.

Jones, Gregory L. "Truth and Consequences in South Africa." *Christianity Today*, April 5, 1999, 59–63.
Kairos Theologians. *The Kairos Document, Challenge to the Church: A Theological Comment on the Political Crisis in South Africa.* Grand Rapids: Eerdmans, 1986.
Kallas, James. "Romans XIII. 1–7: An Interpolation." *NTS* 11 (1965) 365–74.
Kant, Immanuel. *Critique of Pure Reason.* Translated by Norman Kemp Smith. London: Macmillan, 1934.
Käsemann, Ernst. *Commentary on Romans.* Grand Rapids: Eerdmans, 1980.
Kendall, Frances and Leon Louw. *After Apartheid: The Solution for South Africa.* San Francisco: ICS, 1987.
Kitschoff, M. C., and W. B. Van Wyk. *Method of Religious Education and Biblical Studies.* Cape Town: Maskew Miller Longman, 1983.
Kretzschmar, L. *The Voice of Black Theology in South Africa.* Johannesburg: Ravan, 1986.
Krog, Antjie. "The Truth and Reconciliation Commission: A National Ritual." *Missionalia* 26 (1998) 7–11.
———. "Parable of the Bicycle." *Mail & Guardian*, Feb. 7, 1997, 1–5.
Kung, Hans. "Dialogability and Steadfastness: On Two Complementary Virtues, Radical Pluralism and Truth," translated by Marianne Klein. In *Radical Pluralism and Truth: David Tracy and the Hermeneutics of Religion*, edited by Werner G. Jeanrond and Jennifer L. Rike, 237–249. New York: Crossroad, 1991.
Lash, Nicholas. "What Authority Has Our Past?" In *Theology on the Way to Emmaus*, 54. London: SCM, 1986.
Levison, John R. and Priscilla Pope-Levison. "Global Perspectives on New Testament Interpretation." In *Hearing the New Testament: Strategies for Interpretation*, edited by Joel B. Green, 329–348. 1995. Reprinted, Eugene, OR: Wipf & Stock, 2004.
Lombaard, Christo. "The Left Governing Hand and the Right Governing Hand: Begging for a Church without Public Hands?" *JTSA* 109 (2001) 17–22.
Lubbe, Gerrie. "Religious Pluralism and Christianity in South Africa," In *Christianity Amidst Apartheid for Christianity in South Africa*, edited by Martin Prozesky, 208–16. New York: St. Martin's, 1990.
Lundin, Roger, Anthony C. Thiselton, and Clarence Walhout. *Responsibility of Hermeneutics.* Grand Rapids: Eerdmans, 1985.
MacCrone, I. D. "The Frontier Tradition and Race Attitudes." *Race Relations Journal* 28 (1961) 19–30.
Maluleke, Tinyiko Sam. "Dealing Lightly With the Wound of My People: The TRC Process in Theological Perspective." *Missionalia* 25 (1997) 324–43.
———. "Truth, National Unity and Reconciliation in South Africa: Aspects of the Emerging Theological Agenda." *Missionalia* 25 (1997) 59–88.
Majeke, Nosipho. *The Role of the Missionaries in Conquest.* Cape Town, 1986.
Marshall, Howard I. "Introduction." In *New Testament Interpretation: Essays on Principles and Methods*, edited by I. Howard Marshall, 11–20. 1977. Reprint, Eugene, OR: Wipf & Stock, 2006.
Martin, Paul J. "Christianity and Islam: Lessons from Africa." *BYULR* (1998) 401–20.
Marx, Karl, and Friedrich Engels. *Basic Writings on Politics and Philosophy.* Garden City, NJ: Doubleday, 1959.

Mbali, Zolile. *The Churches and Racism: A Black South African Perspective.* London: SCM, 1987.
Mbiti, John. "The Bible in African Culture." In *Paths of African Theology,* edited by Rosino Gibellini, 27-39. New York: Orbis, 1994.
McDonald, J. I. H. "Romans 13:1-7: A Test Case for New Testament Interpretation." *NTS* 35 (1989) 540-49.
McGovern, Arthur F. *Liberation Theology and Its Critics: Toward an Assessment.* Maryknoll: Orbis, 1989.
Mickelsen, Berkeley A. *Interpreting the Bible.* Grand Rapids: Eerdmans, 1963.
Minear, Paul. *The Obedience of Faith: The Purposes of Paul in the Epistle to the Romans.* London: SCM, 1971.
Minow, Martha. "Between Vengeance and Forgiveness: South Africa's Truth and Reconciliation Commission." *Negotiation Journal* (1998) 320-35.
Moller, Francois Petrus. *Church and Politics: A Pentecostal View of the South African Situation.* Johannesburg: Gospel, 1986.
Moodie, Donald. *The Record; or, a Series of Official Papers Relative to the Condition and Treatment of the Native Tribes of South Africa.* 3 volumes. Amsterdam: Balkema, 1960.
Moodie, Dunbar T. *The Rise of Afrikanerdom: Power, Apartheid, and the Afrikaner Civil Religion.* Los Angeles: University of California Press, 1975.
Morris, Leon. *The Epistle to the Romans.* Grand Rapids: Eerdmans, 1992.
Morrison, Clinton Dawson. *The Powers That Be: Earthly Rulers and Demonic Powers in Romans 13,1-7.* Naperville, IL: Allenson, 1960.
Muller-Fahrenholz, Geiko. *The Art of Forgiveness: Theological Reflections on Healing and Reconciliation.* Geneva: WCC Publications, 1996.
Nanos, Mark D. *The Mystery of Romans: The Jewish Context of Paul's Letter.* Minneapolis: Fortress, 1996.
Nederduitse Gereformeerde Kerk. Algemene Sinode. *Human Relations and the South African Scene in the Light of Scripture.* Cape Town: Dutch Reformed Church Publishers, 1976.
Neufeld, Matthew G. "Submission to Governing Authorities: A Study of Romans 13:1-7." *Direction* 23 (1994) 90-97.
Niebuhr, Reinhold. *The Nature and Destiny of Man.* New York: Scribner, 1941.
Oakes, Dougie and Alfie Steyn, editors. *Illustrated History of South Africa–The Real Story.* 3rd ed. Cape Town: Reader's Digest Association, 1994.
Ogle, Arthur B. "What is Left for Caesar: A Look at Mark 12:13-17 and Romans 13:1-7." *ThTo* 35 (1978) 254-64.
Omar, D. "Introduction to the Truth and Reconciliation Commission." In *To Remember and to Heal: Theological and Psychological Reflections on Truth and Reconciliation,* edited by H. Russel Botman and Robin M. Petersen. Cape Town: Human & Rousseau, 1996.
O'Neill, J.C. *Paul's Letter to the Romans.* London: Penguin, 1975.
Pobee, John S., editor. *Religion in a Pluralistic Society.* Leiden: Brill, 1976.
———. *Toward an African Theology.* Nashville: Abingdon, 1979.
Pope-Levison, Priscilla, and John R. Levison. *Jesus in Global Contexts.* Louisville: Westminster John Knox, 1992.

Porter, Stanley. "Romans 13:1–7: As Pauline Political Rhetoric." *Filogia Neo Testamentica* 2 (1990) 115–39.

Porter, Stanley E. and David Tombs, editors. *Approaches to the New Testament Study*. JSNTSup 120. Sheffield: Sheffield Academic, 1995.

Prozesky, Martin editor. *Christianity Amidst Apartheid*. New York: St. Martin's, 1990.

Ratzinger, Joseph Cardinal, with Vittorio Messori. *The Ratzinger Report: An Exclusive Interview on the State of the Church*. Translated by Salvator Attansio and Graham Harrison. San Francisco: Ignatius, 1985.

"Recalling District Six." No Pages. Accessed October 1, 2007. Online: http://www.southafrica.info/ess_info/sa_glance/history/districtsix.htm.

Sanders, Mark. "Loss of Ubuntu: Reconciliation, Ethics, and the Invention of Cultural Memory." No pages. Accessed March 2001. Online: http://www.celat.ulaval.ca/celat/histoire.memoire/histoire/cape1/sanders.htm.

Schillebeeckx, Edward. "Foreword." In *Constructing Local Theologies*, by Robert J. Schreiter, ix–x. Maryknoll, NY: Orbis, 1985.

Schubeck, Thomas L. *Liberation Ethics: Sources, Models, and Norms*. Minneapolis: Fortress, 1993.

Sebidi, L. J. "A Critical Analysis of the Dynamics of the Black Struggle in South Africa and its Implications for Black Theology." Unpublished Paper, 1984.

Sherman, Amy L. *Preferential Option: A Christian Neoliberal Strategy for Latin America's Poor*. Grand Rapids: Eerdmans, 1992.

Shillington, Kevin. *History of Africa*. New York: St. Martin's, 1994.

Shriver, Donald W. *An Ethic for Enemies: Forgiveness in Politics*. New York: Oxford University Press, 1995.

Simkhovitch, Vladimir Grigorievitch. *Toward the Understanding of Jesus*. New York: Macmillan, 1923.

Simpson, Theo "Christianity, Religion and other Religions." *JTSA* 60 (1987) 3–12.

Sipho, Siso Gift. "Confess your Crimes." *New African* (1994) 33.

Smith, Gordon. "Protecting the Weak: Religious Liberty in the Twenty First Century." *BYULR* 2 (1999) 479–502.

Smith, Tim. "A Nation Examines its Conscience." *America*, Nov. 8, 1997, 20–28.

Song, Choan-Seng. *Jesus, the Crucified People*. Minneapolis: Fortress Press, 1996.

———. *Third-Eye Theology: Theology in Formation in Asian Settings*. Rev. ed. New York: Orbis, 1991.

Sparks, Allister. *The Mind of South Africa*. New York: Knopf, 1990.

Stein, Robert H. "The Argument of Romans 13:1–7." *NovT* 31 (1989) 325–43.

Storey, Peter. "A Different Kind of Justice: Truth and Reconciliation in South Africa." *The Christian Century* 114 (1997) 788–91, 793.

Stuhlmacher, Peter. *Paul's Letter to the Romans: A Commentary*. Translated by Scott J. Hafemann. Louisville: WJKP, 1994.

Tate, Randolph W. *Biblical Interpretation*. Peabody: Hendrickson, 1997.

Thiselton, Anthony C. *The Two Horizons: New Testament Hermeneutics and Philosophical Description with Special Reference to Heidegger, Bultmann, Gadamer, and Wittgenstein*. Grand Rapids: Eerdmans, 1980.

Tombs, David. "The Hermeneutics of Liberation." In *Approaches to New Testament Study*, JSNTSup 120, edited by Stanley E. Porter and David Tombs, 310–355. Sheffield: Sheffield Academic, 1995.

———. *Latin American Liberation Theology*. Religion in the Americas 1. Boston: Brill, 2002.

Torrens, James S. "The Many Faces of Amnesty." *America*, July 17, 1999, 12–17.

Truth and Reconciliation Commission of South Africa. *Truth and Reconciliation Commission of South Africa Report*. New York: Palgrave Macmillan, 1999.

Tutu, Desmond. "Between a Nightmare and a Dream: If Reconciliation can Happen in South Africa, It can Happen Elsewhere." *Christianity Today*, Feb. 9, 1998, 25–26.

———. *No Future Without Forgiveness*. New York: Doubleday, 1999.

Van Jaarsveld, F.A. "The Afrikaner's Idea of His Calling and Mission in South African History." *JTSA* 19 (1977) 16–19.

———. *The Awakening of Afrikaner Nationalism: 1868–1881*. Cape Town: Human & Rousseau, 1961.

Van der Vyver, Johan D. "Constitutional Perspective of Church–State Relations in South Africa." *BYULR* 2 (1999) 635–72.

Villa-Vicencio, Charles. *Between Christ and Caesar: Classic and Contemporary Texts on the Church and State*. Grand Rapids: Eerdmans, 1986.

Walls, Andrew F. "Towards Understanding Africa's Place in Christian History." In *Religion in a Pluralistic Society*, edited by C. G. Baëta and John S. Pobee, 180–189. Leiden: Brill, 1976.

Walshe, Peter. *Church Versus State in South Africa: The Case of the Christian Institute*. Maryknoll: Orbis, 1983.

Weissbrodt, David and Paul W. Fraser. "Report of The Chilean National Commission on Truth and Reconciliation." *Human Rights Quarterly* 14 (1992) 601–22.

"Where is World Conscience?" Editorial, *Dawn: The Internet Edition*, March 9, 2002. http://www.dawn.com/2002/03/09/ed.htm.

Witte, John, Jr. "A Most Mild and Equitable Establishment of Religion: John Adams and the Massachusetts Experiment." *JChSt* 41 (1999) 213–52.

Yoder, John Howard. *The Politics of Jesus*. 2nd ed. Grand Rapids: Eerdmans, 1994.

www.ingramcontent.com/pod-product-compliance
Lightning Source LLC
Chambersburg PA
CBHW062046220426
43662CB00010B/1668